In memory
who taugh
importance of traditions.
In memory of my father Horst Schiel,
who loved home cooked meals
and never forgot a holiday.

To my husband Mark, and my
children Steven and Cheryl,
for appreciating German food.
With special thanks to Cheryl,
for her help creating this book.

Table of Contents

Einleitung (Introduction)

This book is for all people who love Germany, our traditions, and good, rich food. It is also for all the people who have never heard of our traditions and have never tasted our food, but would like to discover something new. The recipes in this book have been in my family for generations, and the traditions mentioned are celebrated all over Germany in essentially the same way.
To begin, let me offer a few words about the German meals and etiquette.

Das Frühstück (Breakfast)

Breakfast includes an assortment of breads and rolls. During the week, we choose from lunchmeat, cheese, jelly, cold cereals, yoghurt, curd, and fruit. We have hot chocolate, coffee or tea with honey. During the winter, we add hot cereals, and on weekends, we prepare eggs to complete our breakfast.
A children's favorite is Nutella, a chocolate hazelnut spread.

Das Mittagessen (Lunch)

Lunchtime is usually at about 1:00p.m. This is the time when the children return home from school and have time to eat. German schools do not have a cafeteria, so the children have a break between 1:00p.m and 2:00p.m, and then return to school for afternoon lessons. For almost all children, the school is within walking distance from home; if not, the children take a cold lunch, and have a warm dinner later.

Lunch is a warm meal. It includes meat, vegetables or salads, with potatoes, rice, or noodles. On Fridays, many Germans eat fish. Saturday's lunch is often a simple meal because we are busy cleaning "Haus und Hof" (house and yard).
A complete meal with an appetizer and dessert is served when guests are invited, on holidays, or for special celebrations.

Das Abendessen (Dinner)

Dinnertime depends on the time everybody gets home from work and school. We eat sandwiches and salads like noodle salad or potato salad. Dinner is usually a cold meal. Since many of us eat the main, hot meal around 1:00 p.m., the evening meal is not a grand affair. However, if it is stormy or very cold outside, we might add a hot soup or broth to the meal.

Der Nachmittagskaffee (Afternoon Coffee)

I must not forget the fourth time we eat, the very important afternoon coffee. During the week, it is usually just a quick cup of coffee taken wherever we are, but Sunday afternoons, when family and friends have time to get together, is the best time to have a good cup of coffee with cake or sweets. The time spent together is flexible, but it is usually late afternoon to early evening. If an acquaintance invites us for coffee, we will arrive at 3:00p.m. and stay until about 5:00p.m. If we stay longer, the host might feel obligated to serve dinner as well. If, on the other hand, the coffee is with family or good friends . . .

Brot, Käse, Wurst (Bread, cheese, lunchmeat)

Here is a little information about the three most important items served at so many of our meals: Brot, Käse, and Wurst.
Germany has about two hundred different kinds of bread. Rye breads are at the top of the list with about seventy kinds. The others are wheat, oat, or mixed breads like seven or ten grain. However, all breads have a hard crust and a chewy inside. There are also fifty kinds of rolls, from hard rolls, to sweet rolls, to hearty rolls with onions and other spices. There are several reasons for this enormous diversity. One is that many types of grain, such as wheat, spelt and rye, are native to Germany. Another is that German bakers complete a high standard, creative

training, which most other countries do not have. Following is an image inside a typical German bakery.

Germany is the third biggest exporter of cheese in the world. Some popular kinds are Gouda, Emmentaler, Camenbert, Limburger, Mainzer Käse, and the famous Handkäse.

There are about three hundred kinds of lunchmeats and other meat specialties from which to choose. Many are famous around the world, including the Frankfurter Würstchen, Bratwurst, Liverwurst, and the Weisswurst from Munich. Munich has its own tradition for its beloved Weisswurst. They say, Wurst is not supposed to hear the ringing of the church bells at noon; it should be enjoyed before noon with sweet mustard.

Ettquette:

Die Einladung (The Invitation)

The invitation is the important part of any gathering. Whatever we do, we never go to a party, coffee, dinner, or any other function uninvited. We do not even visit a family member, unless we call first. Generally, the invitation is given verbally unless it is a formal function.

We will RSVP, so the host knows for how many people she/he must plan. As a thank you, we will bring a small gift like candy, flowers, or a bottle of wine to the gathering. The only time we do not bring a gift is when visiting family or very close friends, unless it is their birthday or Christmas. However, we will offer to help with the preparations or the cleanup.

This might seem very restrained to many people, but Germans are used to a very structured form of living, and like things to be organized. However, we have our moments here and there. We might even have a spontaneous pizza party with no invitation needed.

About the Recipes

Use only unsalted butter in the recipes. This is especially important for the Christmas cookies. We like to control the amount of salt used in a recipe, which is easier to do with unsalted butter, and we do like the flavor it brings to a dish.

German Quark (also called curd) has a similar flavor to cottage cheese but has a very smooth texture. Quark is a big part of German nutrition; it is healthy, low on calories, rich in calcium and can be used in many recipes because of its neutral flavor.

Many Germans who live in the U.S. have a Quark maker in which they can make Quark from whole milk. In some states, Quark is also available in grocery stores or specialty stores. It is hard to find a substitution for Quark; cottage cheese can be used or perhaps cream cheese. However, the results will not be quite the same because these cheeses cannot match the velvety texture of Quark.

German Holidays

Karneval (Mardi Gras)

Karneval is also known as Fasching, Fastnacht, or Fasnet, depending on the region and dialect. Outside Europe, it is often called Mardi Gras. We owe many of our Karneval traditions to the pre-Christian Roman times. The Romans brought festivities to the settlements in Cologne, Bonn, Mainz, and Wiesbaden, all of which are now cities along the Rhine. In Roman times, after the ice on the river melted, a festival of ships was celebrated. It was called "Carrus Navalis," which means ship wagon and this is how Karneval originated. This story is reflected in the modern day parades, in which the floats are on wheels like ship wagons.

As a celebration accepted by the Catholic Church, Karneval became a movable holiday, which means the first day of Karneval depends on the beginning of Lent, and Easter Sunday. For six days, from Thursday to Ash Wednesday, anything goes. We start with "Alt Weiberfastnacht" (old women's Fasching) on Thursday, where women have the right to play pranks, like cutting off men's ties as trophies. Traditionally, women wear masks and old clothes making them look very old, almost like witches. The Beueler laundresses started this tradition in 1824. One day a year, the Beueler laundries were closed, usually on the Thursday before Mardi Gras. In 1824, the laundresses united, called themselves "Old Ladies Committee of 1824" and decided to participate in the previously all-male carnival.

On Friday, Saturday, and Sunday, many Karneval gatherings are organized by the Fool's Guild, which is an organization that starts planning the festivities as early as November. Humorous rhyming speech known as Die Büttenrede accompanies the gatherings. Many speeches are political and mock local and national politicians, celebrities, and events. The speakers are usually members of the Fool's Guild.

The Rose Monday parades are broadcast on German television. The parades are similar to Thanksgiving Day parades, but with colorful masks and costumes. Rose Monday is a school holiday and the Fool's Guild organizes gatherings, many of them held on Monday afternoon for the children. They are filled with fun, games, and dancing.

Finally, there is Fasching Tuesday (Shrove Tuesday), the last chance to party until midnight. At midnight, all celebrations end, the music stops, the masks are taken off, and Ash Wednesday begins. Germans also call Karneval "die fünfte Jahreszeit" (the fifth season). The official greeting during this time is Hellau or Alaaf, again depending on the region or dialect, and it means, "have a good and fun day."

On page 8, my parents having fun at a Faschings party (in 1988), and above the Rose Monday parade in Mainz.

The food during the fifth season is very rich and often deep-fried. We try to enjoy everything before Lent starts and forty days of fasting begin. Everybody should try the following pastry at least eat once during Karneval. The Kreppel tastes the best when it is freshly made.

Kreppel

2 cups flour
2¼ tsp. dry yeast
½ cup warm milk
2 tbsp. oil
2 egg yolks
½ tsp. salt
½ cup raspberry jelly
½ cup confectioner's sugar
Oil for deep-frying

- Pour the flour in a large bowl. Mix in the yeast, followed by half the milk and half the sugar.
- Cover and let rise in a warm place for 15 minutes.
- Add the rest of the milk and sugar, oil, egg yolks, and salt.
- Mix well, cover and let rise for 20 minutes.
- Roll the dough out 1 inch thick, and cut out 3 inch circles. There should be an even amount.

- Put a teaspoon of jelly on a circle, set a second circle on top, and press edges together. Fill all the circles this way, cover, and let rise for 15 minutes.
- Deep fry in 350° F oil on each side for 3 minutes.
- Set the Kreppel on a paper towel to remove excess oil.
- Sprinkle with confectioner's sugar.

Osterzeit (Easter Season)

Palmsonntag (Palm Sunday)

The Easter week starts with Palm Sunday. Many families attend a church service. Before church, the congregation meets outside near the church, and everybody receives a blessed palm leaf. The priest then leads the parishioners into the church, singing and celebrating Jesus's arrival in Jerusalem.
Traditionally, the palm leaves are taken home and many families use them to create a crucifix, which they keep throughout the year. The following year, those palm leafs will be burned and their ashes used on Ash Wednesday.

Gründonnerstag (Green Thursday)

Green Thursday is a day of belief and a little superstition. It is a day on which remorseful sinners are welcomed back into the church for communion. Most Christian churches hold a 5:00p.m. Service, with a foot washing ceremony, in memory of the last supper. It is also a day of house cleaning and a day for green foods, like spinach, cabbage, leeks, and chives. We trust the green foods will keep us healthy during the year.
Each region has its own green recipe, but "Sieben Kräuter Suppe" is famous everywhere.

Sieben Kräuter Suppe (Seven Herb Soup)

3 cloves garlic chopped
5 shallots chopped
2 large leeks chopped
¼ tsp. nutmeg
2 cups fresh spinach
3 cups fresh parsley leaves
2 cups mixed greens, chives, cress, sorrel
8 cubs chicken broth
½ cup sour cream
¼ tsp. black pepper
2 tbsp. lemon juice
⅓ cup olive oil

- Heat olive oil in a large pot on medium heat.
- Add shallots, garlic, leeks, and nutmeg, and sauté until the shallots are translucent. Turn down heat to low.
- Add all the other greens and 3 cups of broth. Cook for 4 minutes.
- Put the mixture in a blender and puree until smooth.
- Return mixture to pot and add 5 cups of broth. Bring to a boil.
- Turn heat to low and stir in the sour cream and pepper.
- Take of the heat and add the lemon juice. Serve.

Here is the recipe for my family's Gründonnerstag dinner, which consists of Frankfurter Grüne Sosse and potatoes instead of soup.

Frankfurter Grüne Sosse (Frankfurter Green Sauce)

3 cups mixed herbs (such as parsley, chives, chervil, dill, borage, watercress, basil)

5 hardboiled eggs chopped
3 bread and butter pickles chopped
1 cup of sour cream or plain yogurt
4 tbsp. heavy cream (milk can be used instead)
2 tbsp. mayonnaise
¼ tsp. pepper
¼ tsp. salt
1 tsp. fresh lemon juice
1 tsp. sugar

- Blend sour cream, heavy cream, mayonnaise, pepper, salt, sugar, and lemon juice until smooth.
- Stir in eggs and pickles.
- Thoroughly rinse herbs, pat dry, and chop. Blend with the sauce.
- Serve over baked potatoes.

Karfreitag (Good Friday)

The name Karfreitag (Good Friday) comes from the Old High German form of kara, which means care. In some regions, the day is also known as Stiller Freitag (quiet Friday).

In the Roman Catholic Church, no bells are rung; in fact, many children believe the bells are flown to Rome to be blessed. It was an imaginative explanation why the bells were not rung. There are countless church services on Karfreitag, many of them start at noon and last until 3 p.m., which is, according to Matthew 27:45-54, the hours of Jesus Christ's crucifixion and death. St. Matthews Passion by Bach and other Passion plays are performed during the service.

Numerous workplaces close on this day, but employees who do work, have the right to visit a service if they wish. Overall, it is a very solemn day. Most families have fish for their main meal. Before the meal, twigs are brought into the house, and left bare for the day as a reminder of the crown of thorns. The next day, Easter Saturday, these twigs will be transformed into the Easter tree.

Here is a fish dish for Karfreitag:

Barsch mit Kräuter (Perch with Herbs)

4 large perch fillets
1 tsp. salt
½ tsp. pepper
6 bay leaves crumbled
2 tbsp. sage chopped
2 tbsp. rosemary chopped
Juice of one lemon
2 tbsp. olive oil
3 tbsp. butter
2 tbsp. parsley chopped

- Preheat oven to 425° F.
- Make a paste of salt, pepper, bay leaves, sage, rosemary, olive oil, and lemon juice.
- Spread paste equally on 4 perch fillets.
- Line baking sheet with parchment paper.
- Put fillets on baking sheet, dot with butter, and sprinkle parsley on top.
- Bake at 425° F for 10 minutes.
- Serve with potato salad.

Ostersamstag (Easter Saturday)

Most families are busy finishing the decorations and preparing the food for Sunday. Children make little nests of straw for the Osterhase (Easter bunny), so he knows where to put the eggs. Parents will hide the nests or store bought baskets, inside or outside the house, depending on the weather.

Eggs are the symbol for fertility and a new beginning. Blown eggs are painted and decorated for the Easter tree, which is transformed from the twigs and symbolizes joy and the end of Jesus's suffering.

Bouquets of Daffodils, known as Osterglocke (Easter bells) in Germany, are spread throughout the house. Having an Easter bonfire on Saturday night just before the Easter mass is a widespread tradition. The bonfire is a sign of Christ's resurrection; it also symbolizes the driving out of the darkness of winter and the coming of warmth. In Catholic regions, the bonfire is near the church and is blessed. During a prayer, the priest will light the Easter candle from the fire, and each parishioner will then light a small candle from the flame from the Easter candle. They then form a procession into the church for the midnight service.

Ostersonntag (Easter Sunday)

Ostersonntag usually starts with the children searching for the hidden Easter nests, which are now filled with chocolate bunnies, marzipan, eggs, and other goodies. Sometimes a small present, like a book or a stuffed animal (usually a bunny), is found in the nest.

Families will gather at the church for Sunday morning mass, and afterwards for a late breakfast. Many towns have folk festivals, and if the weather is nice, an Osterspaziergang (a walk) is taken to search for the first spring flowers.

Monday is also an official holiday in most European countries, because according to the bible, Jesus rose on the third day, which is Monday.

I am looking for Easter eggs in 1966.

Friends and families come together for a festive dinner on either Sunday or Monday. Many different Easter menus are designed for these occasions; here is one example:

- Königssuppe
- Kräuterlamm mit Kroketten, und Rotkraut
- Eiscreme Kuchen

Königssuppe (Kings Soup)

1 lb. beef chunk cross cuts
3 cups water (to start)
1½ tsp. salt
1 leek stalk sliced
1 celery stalk sliced
1 large carrot sliced
1 small onion chopped
2 tomatoes chopped
¼ tsp. garlic powder
Salt, nutmeg, and fresh chopped parsley to taste

Also:
2 eggs
6 tbsp. milk
2 tbsp. water
½ tsp. salt
¼ tsp. nutmeg
Butter for form

- Bring water and salt to a boil.
- Simmer beef chunks, vegetables, salt, and garlic powder for 2½ hours.
- Pour soup through a sieve until it is a clear bouillon.
- Add spices and chopped parsley.
- **Start eggs 1 hour before soup is done.**
- Preheat oven to 300° F.
- Scramble eggs with milk, water, salt, and nutmeg.
- Butter a small oven safe dish and pour in eggs.
- Set covered dish in a roasting pan with boiling water
- Bake for 45 minutes.
- Take eggs out of the dish, cut in small stripes, and add to bouillon.
- Serve.

Kräuterlamm (Herbed Lamb)

1 leg of lamb boned
6 tbsp. fresh parsley
6 tbsp. fresh thyme
3 tbsp. fresh oregano
4 tbsp. fresh rosemary
4 tbsp. dried mustard
6 gloves of garlic
¾ cup olive oil
2 cups red wine
Several sprigs of fresh rosemary

- Grind all spices, excluding the sprigs of rosemary in the food processor.

- Add wine and oil and blend until it is a smooth liquid.
- Pour marinade over meat and refrigerate for 24 to 48 hours, turning occasionally.
- Put lamb onto a roasting pan and bake in a preheated oven at 425° F for 15 minutes. Reserve 2 cups of the marinade.
- Turn oven down to 325° F, add sprigs of rosemary on top, and cook for 15 minutes per pound.
- Baste with marinade every 20 minutes.
- Lamb should be pink in the middle; for better-done meat add 5 minutes per pound.

Kroketten (Potato Tots)

1½ lb. potatoes peeled, washed and quartered
2 tbsp. butter
2 eggs
3 tbsp. flour
¼ tsp. nutmeg
½ tsp. salt
Also:
1 tbsp. milk
1½ cups of breadcrumbs
Oil for deep-frying

- Cook potatoes until done, drain and let cool.
- Mash cooled potatoes until no lumps remain.
- Add butter, 1 egg, flour, salt, and nutmeg.
- Mix well.
- Form a ½-inch thick roll. Cut roll into 1½-inch pieces.
- Scramble 1 egg with 1 tbsp. of milk
- Roll pieces first into egg/milk mixture, then in breadcrumbs.
- Deep fry until golden brown.

The **Rotkraut** (purple cabbage) is available in all supermarkets and is simply reheated. If you would like to make Rotkraut yourself, you will find the recipe on page 130.

Eiskreme Kuchen (Ice-cream Cake)

For the cake:
8 egg yolks
7 tbsp. sugar
4 egg white
3 tbsp. all-purpose flour
2 tbsp. cornstarch
1 tbsp. baking cocoa
For the filling:
6 egg whites
⅔ cup sugar
1 tsp. baking cocoa
2 tbsp. red currant jelly
Half-gallon of Napoleon ice cream

- Beat 4 egg whites with half of the sugar until a stiff peak forms, set aside.
- Mix egg yolks with the rest of the sugar.
- In a bowl, layer egg yolk mixture, dried ingredients, and egg white mixture. Mix very carefully with a wooden spoon until combined.
- Do not use an electric mixer, it adds to much air to the cake.
- Preheat oven to 400° F.
- Pour cake mix into an 8x8 inch baking pan and bake for 12 minutes.
- Remove cake from pan, let cool completely.
- Cut the cooled cake into the form of the ice cream block.
- Beat egg whites, sugar, and cocoa until a stiff peak forms.
- Preheat oven to 400° F.

- Spread jelly on cake and set the ice cream block on top.
- Cover cake with egg white mixture.
- Bake until golden brown.
- Serve right away.

Walpurgisnacht (Walpurgis Night)

Walpurgisnacht is the night of April 30th to May 1st. It is named after Saint Walpurga, a woman who was born in England in 710 and traveled to Germany at a young age to become a nun at a convent in Heidelberg. The Catholic Church named this day after a Saint to take away the pagan character of this pre-Christian spring festival. Walpurga is the patron Saint of seafaring and against evil spirits. Each year, the clouds and fog and mysterious atmosphere of the Brocken, the highest peak of the Harz Mountains, proves perfect for gatherings. Here, the Hexen (witches) assemble and dance, just like in Goethe's Faust,"To the Brocken the witches ride . . . " All night, these witches and other practitioners of the occult celebrate the beginning of spring before they are banished at sunrise. For the rest of us who cannot ride to the Brocken there is always a "Tanz in den Mai" (dance into May). Most towns have a celebration to welcome May, not only with dancing, but also with a very special wine.

Maibowle (May Punch)

1 cup of Waldmeister (woodruff)
¾ cup sugar
3 bottles white wine (a good Riesling)
1 bottle Champagne
- Mix sugar and 1 chilled bottle wine.
- Add woodruff, and let stand for 1 hour.

- Remove woodruff and add 2 bottles wine and Champagne.
- Serve.

Tag der Arbeit (Labor day)

This is the first day of May and a national holiday across Europe. Many families use the day for picnicking and relaxing; others visit union meetings and listen to political speeches.

In larger cities, demonstrations take place, usually about work related issues. Sadly, sometimes the demonstrations end in clashes between demonstrators and the police.

In rural areas, the Maibaum (May pole), a tall wooden pole with colorful ribbons, flowers, and carved regional decorations is raised. The town's population comes together for the ceremonial raising of the Maibaum, which is usually in the Public Square or marketplace. Festivities follow with Wurst and beer and dancing around the Maibaum.

A typical Maibaum.

Muttertag (Mother's day)

Muttertag is on the second Sunday in May. Like most countries, German mothers will receive little surprises, including breakfast in bed.
Here is a simple and delicious Muttertag cake for the afternoon coffee:

Himbeerkuchen (Raspberry Cake)

1½ cups all-purpose flour
½ tsp. salt
8 tbsp. cold butter
2 tbsp. whipping cream
½ cup sugar
3 cups fresh raspberries
For the topping:
1 cup sugar
1 tbsp. all-purpose flour
2 eggs beaten
1 cup whipping cream
1 tsp. vanilla extract

- Preheat oven to 375° F and grease a 9x13 inch pan.
- Combine 1 cup of flour with the salt, cut in the butter, and blend until the mixture resembles coarse crumbs.
- Stir in cream and pat dough into prepared pan.
- Combine sugar and remaining flour and sprinkle over crust.
- Arrange raspberries on top.
- For the topping, combine sugar and flour. Stir in eggs, cream, and vanilla and pour the mixture over the berries.
- Bake for about 40 minutes until slightly browned.
- Serve warm or chilled. Store in the refrigerator.

Christi Himmelfahrt (Ascension Day)

Forty days after Easter, we celebrate the ascension of Jesus to his Father in Heaven. This day has also become Father's Day, when this happened exactly is not quite clear. However, it is a public holiday, and it allows fathers to enjoy a day without duties.

Pfingsten (Pentecost)

On the seventh Sunday after Easter, we remember the Holy Ghost's decent and the beginning of the apostle's missionary work. Pfingstmonntag (Pentecost Monday) is also holiday. Most families just enjoy the time off because this is the last public holiday until the fall.

My sister Daniela, and cousins Achim and Thomas on Pfingsten in 1963.

This is my favorite recipe for Pfingsten:

Krautrouladen (Cabbage Rolls)

1 large head cabbage
1 lb. ground chuck

⅓ cup instant rice, cooked
1 small onion grated
2 eggs
1 tsp. salt
¼ tsp. pepper
1 large onion sliced
1 – 15 oz. can tomato sauce
3 – 15 oz. cans diced tomatoes
4 tsp. lemon juice
1 tsp. salt
¼ tsp. pepper
1 cup brown sugar

- Remove about 15 large leaves from the cabbage and cut off the thick stem of each leave.
- Pour boiling water over the leaves to wilt them.
- Preheat oven to 350 degrees F.
- Combine chuck, rice, grated onion, eggs, 1 tsp. salt, and ¼ tsp. pepper.
- Distribute the meat mixture between the 15 cabbage leaves.
- Fold the sides of leave over and roll up.
- In a large casserole dish, place a sliced onion and cabbage rolls in layers with seam side down.
- In a saucepan, mix tomato sauce, diced tomatoes, lemon juice, 1 tsp. salt, and ¼ tsp. pepper.
- Bring sauce to a boil.
- Add brown sugar and pour over cabbage rolls.
- Bake covered for 1 hour, then uncovered for ½ hour.

Mittsommernacht (Midsummer Night)

Many call Mittsommernacht "Johannestag", named after St. John the Baptist. We celebrate this on the shortest night of the year. According to mythology, on midsummer's night we will find hidden treasures and understand the language of the animals. So far, I do not know anybody to whom this has happened, but it is nice to imagine. The true celebrations are the bonfires in public places and the gatherings of friends and family.

In Bavaria, large burning wooden wheels are rolled down the mountains. Along the Rhine, each town is illuminated with a different color that reflects on the water, and gives the impression of the "Rhine on Flames".

Something spectacular: Rhine in Flames.

Many other traditions include dances, games, and food made from the first reaped fresh fruit and vegetables. A refreshing dessert for Mittsommernacht:

Rote Grütze (Red Grits)

½ cup raspberries
½ cup red currant berries
½ cup sour cherries with stones removed
½ cup sugar
4 cups water
4 tbsp. cornstarch
6 tbsp. cold water
Sweetened, Whipped heavy cream for garnish
- Clean and wash all fruit.
- Cook with water and sugar for 10 minutes, stirring every 2 minutes.

- Pour fruits through a strainer, reserving the liquid.
- Mix cornstarch with cold water.
- Bring fruit juice to a boil, add cornstarch, and bring back to a boil.
- Remove from heat and taste to determine if more sugar is needed; if it is, add right away.
- Chill for 6 hours.
- Garnish with Whipped cream before serving.

Siebenschläfer (St. Swithin's Day)

Similar to the groundhog's shadow on Groundhog Day, on June 27, the day of the Siebenschläfer (dormouse), we hope it will not rain; if it does, it will rain for the next seven weeks.

Tag der Deutschen Einheit (Day of German Unity)

After the wall came down in 1989, October 3 became the German National Holiday as, on this day, East and West Germany were officially reunited. Celebrations are similar to Independence Day, but there are no military parades, just festivals and gatherings. It is a day of remembrance.

Erntedank (Harvest Festival of Thanks)

Erntedank is primarily a religious celebration and is always on the first Sunday in October. Farmers give thanks to their good fortune and the abundant harvest from fields and gardens. A harvest altar is set up in churches. Locally available fruit, grains and vegetables are placed around the altar. Many times a center point is made from a cornucopia.

The blessed food will be donated to a soup kitchen, or food pantry, wherever it is most needed.

A typical Erntedank Altar

The German Allgäuer Alps, as well as in Austria and Switzerland have a different tradition called "Almabtrieb", meaning the cattle's return to the valley. This festival sees the cattle that have been feeding on the lush alpine pastures thus producing better milk and cheese return down the mountain for the winter. The cows are covered in flower displays and wear large cowbells around their neck, which can be heard long before the cows are in sight. Locals in traditional costumes return with the cows to make this a colorful spectacle.

Cows on their way to the valley

We do not have a customary dinner on Erntedank. Our gratitude for the filled barns makes the day special. However, families and friends do gather for an evening together.

A creamy, warm soup, and a delicious dessert to celebrate the day:

Käsesuppe (Cheese Soup)

2 tsp. minced garlic
4 tbsp. butter
2 medium onions diced
1 leek in small rings
8 oz. medium sharp Gouda cheese cubed
4 tbsp. flour
4 cups vegetable broth
8 oz. heavy cream
½ tsp. sugar
¼ tsp. salt
¼ tsp. pepper
¼ cup white wine
1 cup plain small croutons

- Melt butter in a large pot.
- Sauté garlic, onions, and leeks.
- Dust with the flour and mix well.

- Add broth and heavy cream, stirring constantly.
- Simmer for 10 minutes.
- Add cheese, sugar, and salt and pepper. Keep stirring.
- When cheese is completely melted, add white wine.
- Garnish with croutons before serving.

Rustikale Birnentarte mit Spätem Riesling
(Rustic Pear Tart with Late-Harvest Riesling)

Crust:
1½ cups all-purpose flour
3 tbsp. sugar
½ tsp. Salt
10 tbsp. chilled unsalted butter, cut into pieces
1 large egg yolk
1 tbsp. late-harvest Riesling or other sweet white dessert wine

- Mix flour, sugar, and salt.
- Mix in butter until mixture resembles coarse a meal.
- Add egg yolk and wine and blend until moist clumps form.
- Form dough into a ball, flatten into a disk, wrap in plastic wrap. Chill from 40 minutes up to 2 days.

Filling:
3 large ripe Anjou pears, peeled, cored and thinly sliced
1 tbsp. sugar
½ cup sugar
1 tbsp. all-purpose flour
1 cup late-harvest Riesling or other sweet white dessert wine
½ cup water
Good vanilla ice cream if desired

- Position rack in center of oven and preheat to 375F.
- Roll chilled dough between two sheets of parchment paper to a 12-inch circle.

- Remove top sheet of paper and transfer dough to backing sheet. Remove rest of paper.
- Place pear slices, 1 tbsp. sugar, and flour in a bowl. Toss to combine.
- Spoon pear mixture into center of dough, leaving 1½-inch border.
- Fold up outer edge of dough over edge of filling.
- Bake pear mixture for about 20 minutes until tender.

Allerheiligen (All Saints Day)

Saints, martyrs, and the dead are honored each year on November 1. The graves and cemeteries are decorated. Catholics light candles at the gravesites, which glow until Allerseelen (All Souls Day) the next day. The candles symbolize the eternal light that provides illumination for the dead.

Sankt Martin (Saint Martin's)

Sankt Martin is a special day for children, but even adults can enjoy the day. We celebrate St. Martin's on November 11, and it is the first sign that the winter holiday season is coming closer.
The best-known legend associated with St. Martin is known as "die Mantelteilung" or the dividing of the cloak. Martin (c.317 – 397) was a Roman soldier and was on his way back to his garrison when he came upon a freezing beggar. Martin tore his cloak in two to share it with the beggar. The following night, God spoke to Martin and thanked him for saving him from the cold. Martin changed his life after that night; he became baptized and served only the church. Later he became Bishop of Tours.
The main festivity on St. Martin's Day is that of making or buying paper lanterns to carry in processions. Schools, Kindergartens, or Churches organize most of these processions and the police stop street traffic to allow the

processions to cross. Often, a mounted police officer or even volunteers dress as a Roman soldier to lead the procession. Most towns' turn the streetlights off in the areas through which the children walk; the glow of the lanterns is enough to guide the way.

Steven and Cheryl are ready for St. Martin (1993). The children gather at St. Hedwigs Church in Wiesbaden.

The children sing many songs, mostly honoring St. Martin or the special meaning of the light.
Here is one:
Ich geh' mit meiner Laterne
Und meine Laterne mit mir.
Da oben leuchten die Sterne,
Hier unten da leuchten wir.

(I'm coming with my lantern
And my lantern with me.
There, above the light are the stars,
Here, under the light are we).

    We also use the day to teach the children about sharing. Many churches or other organizations collect canned goods for the upcoming holiday season. Kindergartens collect toys, and children can choose what they want to share with a less fortunate child.
A special meal on St. Martin's is roast goose.

Martinsgans mit Apfelfüllung (Goose with Apple Stuffing)

1 ready to cook goose (8-10 lbs.)
2 cups water
1 small onion, sliced
1¼ tsp. salt
6 cups soft breadcrumbs
3 tart apples, chopped
2 stalks celery (with leaves), chopped
1 medium onion, chopped
¼ cup butter, melted
2 tsp. salt
1 tsp. ground sage
½ tsp. ground thyme
¼ tsp. pepper
1 tsp. salt
¼ cup all-purpose flour
- Trim excess fat from goose.
- Bring giblets, water, sliced onion, and 1¼ tsp. salt to a boil. Reduce heat, cover, and simmer for 1 hour.
- Strain broth.
- Chop giblets.
- Toss with remaining ingredients except 1 tsp. salt and the flour.

- Rub cavity of goose with 1 tsp. salt; fill goose with stuffing. Fasten opening with skewers and prick skin all over with a fork.
- Place goose breast, side up, on rack in a shallow roasting pan.
- Roast uncovered 2 hours at 350 F; remove excess fat from pan occasionally.
- Cover goose with foil and roast for 1 hour at 350 F.
- Let stand for 15 minutes for easier carving.
- Meanwhile, pour ¼ cup of drippings into a pan. Stir in flour and cook over low heat, stirring constantly until smooth.
- Add another 2 cups of drippings to the pan (add water if needed to make two cups).
- Bring to a boil, stirring constantly.
- Serve goose with the apple stuffing and gravy.

Die Weihnactszeit (The Christmas Season)

In Germany, we call the time from December 1 to December 24 "Weihnachtszeit" or "Adventszeit". Advent starts four Sundays before Christmas Eve and those weeks have many traditions. We reflect on the past year, celebrate, and gather around family and friends. Even though Christmas became somewhat commercialized in recent years, in Germany the holidays retain much of their old charm. Here are some of the customs, which make Christmas in Germany a time to remember.

Der Adventskranz (The Advent Wreath)

A typical Advent wreath is made of evergreen branches, and decorated with red-green ribbon, pinecones, red berries, little stars, and four candles. On the first

Sunday of Advent one candle is lit; on the Second Advent a second candle is lit and so on.

Ideas for traditional Advent wreath

On each Sunday of Advent the family gathers for cookies, carols, and to light another candle. Children have a special countdown:

Advent, Advent …ein Lichtlein brennt
Erst eins, dann zwei, dann drei, dann vier
Dann steht das Christkind for der Tür.
(Advent, Advent …one light is burning
First one, then two, then three, then four
Then the Christ child will stand before our door).

Der Adventskalender (The Advent Calendar)

The Adventskalender is another traditional way to count down the days until Christmas. The calendars are typically made of cardboard and have 24 little flaps or doors. On each day leading up to Christmas, the children open one door behind which a picture with a Christmas scene, a piece of chocolate or a small toy is found. Originally, families made a mark for each of the 24 days with chalk on the wall. The first handcrafted Adventkalendars were produced in the mid-nineteenth century. Today, Adventkalendars are available in every store, although many families have a handcrafted one made of wood or fabric.

Cross-stitched Advents calendar my mother made for us children 45 years ago. Each day had a little package, and we took turns opening them. The other Advents calendar is an example for one a purchased one.

Der Weihnachtsmarkt (The Christmas market)

The start of the Advent season also marks the beginning of Christmas markets. Nearly every town, large or small, has its own market. The streets leading to the town squares are lit with Christmas lights and decorated with Christmas symbols, the squares themselves are buzzing with activity. The aroma of Glühwein (hot mulled wine), baked goods, and other specialties fills the squares. Glühwein actually means, "glow wine", because it warms the body and the spirit from the inside and makes you glow in anticipation of Christmas. Seasonal items, handcrafted toys, baking moulds, and candles are for sale in decorated booths.

Many Christmas markets have a history stretching back 400-years. Each market has its own regional specialty for which it is famous. The Quetschenmännchen (little prune men) and Brenten (almond cookies) of the Frankfurter Christmas market are a must have. Aachen has Aachener Printen (Gingerbread men), Lübeck has Lübecker Marzipan, Dresden has Stollen (fruitcake) and the Erzgebirge is famous for its handmade wooden crafts. Augsburg has a life-size Advent calendar, and the Nürnberger Christkindlmarkt, which is one of the oldest and largest markets, has its famous gold foil angels and Nürnberger Lebkuchen (Gingerbread).

Nürnberger Christkindlmarkt

Here are some Weihnachtsmarkt recipes:

Glühwine (Hot Mulled Wine)

1 bottle of dry red wine (750mL)
1 lemon
2 sticks of cinnamon
3 whole gloves
3 tbsp. sugar
- Heat wine in a pot but do not boil.
- Slice lemon and add to wine.
- Add the rest of the ingredients.
- Heat for 5 minutes but do not boil.
- Take off heat and let stand for one hour.
- Strain, reheat, and serve in pre-warmed mugs.

Glühwein für Kinder (Hot Mulled Wine for Children)

4 cups apple juice
2 cups black tea
2 tbsp. sugar
1 lemon
1 orange
1 cinnamon stick
2 whole gloves
- Slowly heat the apple juice and tea.
- Peel lemon and orange. Reserve the peels.
- Juice the lemon and orange and add juice to heated liquid.
- Add the rest of the ingredients, including lemon and orange peel.
- Continue to heat but do not boil.
- Strain and serve.

Marzipan is a sweet treat made from almonds and sugar and was first mentioned in the Middle East during the fourteenth century. It quickly made its way to Europe and is now one of the main delicatessens during the Christmas season. Marzipan can be found in every possible shape from the original loaf shape, to stars, figurines, animals, and hearts. The most famous Marzipan is made in the city of Lübeck.

Marzipan

3 egg whites
8 ounces blanched almonds
2 cups confectioner's sugar
1 tsp. almond extract
3 drops any food coloring (optional)

- Process almonds in food processor until finely ground.
- Mix ground almonds with egg whites, sugar, and almond extract.
- Knead until dough is smooth and uniform.
- Divide into pieces, color if desired, and shape or use in cookie or cake recipes.

Stollen is a type of German fruitcake using butter, raisins and lemon zest, as the main ingredients. Some variations include marzipan, poppy seeds, and nuts.
The city of Dresden is world famous for its Stollen. Stollen has been sold there since the fifteenth century.
Each year, Dresden celebrates the Stollen festival and the bakers of Dresden produce about 800 lbs. of Stollen and serve it to the visitors.

Dresdner Stollen (Fruitcake)

3 tbsp. raisins
3 tbsp. dried currents
3 ounces candied lemon peel

4 tbsp. Rum
¾ tbsp. active dry yeast
6 tbsp. sugar
1½ tbsp. lukewarm water
4 cups all-purpose flour
½ cup blanched slivered almonds
½ cup milk
½ cup grated lemon zest
½ tsp. salt
1 egg
6 tbsp. butter, diced and softened
¼ cup butter melted
4 tbsp. confectioner's sugar

- Place the fruit in the Rum and soak for one hour.
- Sprinkle 1½ tbsp. flour and the almonds into the fruit and stir until flour is absorbed.
- In a separate bowl, stir the yeast and 1 tsp. sugar into the water. Let stand for 15 minutes.
- Warm the milk until lukewarm. Add lemon peel, almond extract, and the remaining sugar. Stir until sugar has dissolved. Do not bring to a boil.
- Place all but ¼ cup of flour in a large bowl. Add salt, yeast mixture, egg, milk, sugar mixture, and softened butter. Mix to form a smooth dough.
- Turn dough onto a floured surface and knead with the rest of the flour for 15 minutes or until it is no longer sticky.
- Knead in fruit and almond mixture.
- Brush a large bowel with 1 tbsp. melted butter. Place dough in bowel and brush top with 1 tbsp. melted butter. Cover with a clean cloth and let rise for 2 hours.
- Punch down dough. Form to an about 4x14 inch loaf.
- Place loaf on a floured baking sheet.
- Brush with melted butter, and let rest on a warm place for 1 hour, or until doubled in size.
- Bake at 350° F for 45 minutes until golden brown.

- Cool on wire rack. Dust with confectioner's sugar before serving.

December 4 – Barbaratag (Saint Barbara's Day)

Barbara was born at about 280AD, a daughter of very influential and heathenish parents. Barbara believed in God, went to church, and did much good by helping the poor. This upset her father, and, as punishment, he locked her in the basement where she lived on bread and water. Barbara shared the little water she had with the branch of a cherry tree that lay on the basement window. This branch bloomed on Christmas Eve. She refused to abandon her beliefs, and was beheaded by her father in 306AD. Today, Barbara is the guardian angel for firefighters, farmers, and miners.

To honor Barbara, cut a branch of a cherry tree or any other blooming tree, on December 4. Let the branch rest for one night in warm water. Put the branch in a vase; change the water every third day and it might bloom on Christmas Eve.

There is a poem for Barbaratag:

Go to the garden on Barbara day.
Go to the empty cherry tree and say:
Short is the day, grey is the time,
The winter started and spring is far.
But in three weeks it is going to happen.
We celebrate a day more beautiful than spring.
Tree, a branch give me from you,
Even so it is empty I'll take it with me.
And the branch will bloom in shiny magnificence;
In the middle of the winter,
In the nights of the nights,
In the Holy Night.

Original German by Josef Guggenmos

December 6 – Sankt Nikolaus (Saint Nicholas)

The real St. Nicholas lived in the fourth century and was a Bishop in the Asian city of Myra. He was known as a protector of children. He brought food and gifts to them anonymously and saved many children from starving. Nicholas died a highly respected man. Today, he is the guardian angel of schoolchildren and students.
We celebrate his good deeds on December 6· Children put their boots in front of the door the night before; in the morning, they find them filled with cookies, oranges, nuts, some chocolate, and a book, or another small gift. Sometimes St. Nicholas comes in person, with his helper Knecht Ruprecht. Knecht Ruprecht brings a sack of gifts for the good children and a rod for the bad ones. St. Nicholas asks the children if they have been good or bad, he praises them for the things they did well, and talks to them about the things they could do better. A friend or neighbor often dresses up and visits the children in the neighborhood. In Germany, St. Nicholas traditionally comes dressed as a bishop.

St. Nikolaus

Der Tannenbaum (The Christmas Tree)

Traditionally the Christmas tree is put up on Christmas Eve or the day before. It is decorated with glass balls, tinsel, straw ornaments, and sweets. A star or angel tops the tree, and, beside it, a nativity scene might be set up. Many families still use real candles; others use simple white electrical lights. The tree is usually kept until January 6, which is Three Kings Day.
Often children do not see the Weihnachtszimmer (Christmas room) with the tree and the gifts until the afternoon of December 24. The anticipation that their every wish may have come true is sometimes unbearable for them.

December 24 – Heiliger Abend (Christmas Eve)

The day begins as a regular workday, but businesses start to close for the holiday between noon and 2p.m. In Germany, der Heilige Abend (Christmas Eve) is the main focal point of the holiday celebration.
We begin the evening with a family meal. Every family has its own favorite foods. Afterward, the door to the Weihnachtszimmer opens and children see the tree for the first time. Gifts are exchanged followed by the reading of the Christmas gospel. At 8p.m., the bells of every church all over Germany regardless of denomination ring for five minutes in honor of Christ. Bells are broadcast over the radio and families listen to them in a moment of silence. The highpoint of the Heilig Abend celebration is the midnight mass. In addition, some church services are offered at an earlier time for families with small children.

December 25 and 26 – Erste und Zweite Weihnachtstag
(First and Second Christmas Day)

Both days are official holidays in Germany. Businesses are closed, and the time is used to visit family or friends.

Weihnachtsplätzchen (Christmas Cookies)

Zimtsterne (Cinnamon Stars)

3 egg whites
¾ cup sugar
1 tsp. cinnamon
1⅓ cups ground almonds
confectioner's sugar for dusting
- Preheat oven to 250° F and line cookie sheets with parchment paper.
- Whisk egg whites until stiff enough to mark with a knife.
- Gradually add sugar and cinnamon, continuing to mix on a low speed.
- Put aside 3 tbsp. of the egg white mixture.
- Fold in the ground almonds by hand.
- Let the dough rest in the refrigerator for 30 minutes.
- Turn dough onto a surface lightly sprinkled with confectioner's sugar. Roll out until dough is about ¼ inch thick.
- Cut out stars and put them on the cookie sheet.
- Brush tops with the egg whites.
- Bake for 15 to 20 minutes.

Vanillkipferl (Vanilla Crescent)

¾ cup all-purpose flour
½ cup ground almonds
⅓ cup ground hazelnuts
⅓ cup sugar
¾ cup cold butter cut into pieces
2 tsp. vanilla extract
1 egg
1 egg yolk
¼ cup confectioner's sugar.
- Preheat oven to 325° F and line cookie sheets with parchment paper.
- Mix all ingredients together, except the confectioner's sugar.
- Wrap the dough in foil.
- Let the dough rest in the refrigerator for 30 minutes.
- Cut small pieces (the size of a thumb) of the dough and shape each piece into a crescent (kipferl).
- Place on cookie sheet and bake for 8 to 10 minutes.
- Cool for 1 minute and carefully roll in confectioner's sugar.

Kokos Makronen (Coconut Macaroons)

2¾ cups flaked coconut
4 egg whites
1 cup sugar
1 tsp. cinnamon
- Preheat oven to 250° F and line cookie sheets with parchment paper.
- Whisk egg whites until stiff enough to mark with a knife.
- Gradually add sugar and cinnamon, mixing on a low speed.
- Fold in coconut by hand.

- Drop by teaspoonful's onto the prepared cookie sheet.
- Bake for 20 to 25 minutes until cookies are dry and lightly golden.

Honigplätzchen (Honey Cookies)

1 cup butter at room temperature
1 cup sugar
1 cup honey
2 eggs
1 tsp. vanilla extract
1 tsp. baking soda
4 cups all-purpose flour
1 tsp. ground ginger

- Preheat oven to 350° F and line cookie sheets with parchment paper.
- In a medium saucepan over low heat, melt butter, sugar, and honey.
- Pour mixture into a large bowl and let cool to room temperature.
- Mix eggs, vanilla, baking soda, and ginger. Gradually add to the cooled honey mixture.
- Slowly add flour and mix until well blended.
- Drop teaspoonful's on a cookie sheet about 2-inch apart.
- Bake for 12 to 15 minutes until golden brown.

Schneeflocken (Snowflakes)

2 sticks of butter
⅓ cup confectioner's sugar
3 tsp. vanilla extract
⅔ cup all-purpose flour
¾ cup cornstarch

- Preheat oven to 350° F and line cookie sheets with parchment paper.
- Cream the butter.
- Mix in all other ingredients.
- Let the dough rest in the refrigerator for 30 minutes.
- Form 1-inch balls and set them on the cookie sheet. Press them flat with a fork (so the fork marks are visible).
- Bake for 12 to 15 minutes until lightly golden brown.
- Dust the cooled cookies with confectioner's sugar.

Weihnachtssterne (Christmas Stars)

½ cup butter at room temperature
½ cup sugar
1 cup all-purpose flour
1 egg yolk
¼ tsp. fresh lemon juice
Red currant jelly and confectioner's sugar
- Preheat oven to 350° F and line cookie sheets with parchment paper.
- Combine all ingredients, except the jelly and the confectioner's sugar, until smooth.
- Let the dough rest in the refrigerator for 30 minutes.
- Lightly flour a surface and roll dough out to about ¼-inch in thickness.
- Cut out stars and set on a cookie sheet.
- Make a small dent in the middle of the star and fill it with red currant jelly.
- Bake for 12 to 15 minutes.
- Dust with confectioner's sugar when cooled.

Haferflockenplätzchen (Oatmeal Cookies)

6 tbsp. whole milk
1½ sticks of butter
2 tbsp. baking cocoa
1 tsp. vanilla extract
1⅓ cups quick cooking oatmeal
1 tsp. white Rum or rum flavor

- Line cookie sheets with parchment paper.
- In a medium saucepan, melt butter, sugar, cocoa, and vanilla.
- Bring to a boil and remove immediately from heat.
- Stir in oatmeal and Rum.
- Drop teaspoonful's on cookie sheets.
- Let the cookies dry overnight.

And here we end the old year and begin a new one:

Silvester (New Year's Eve)

We celebrate the change of the year merrily and noisily with family and friends. Named after Silvester, a Roman priest, the last night of the year is filled with tradition.

A popular Silvester custom is known as "Bleigiessen". A small piece of lead is put on a spoon, melted over a flame, and dropped into a bowl of cold water. The shape tells your fortune for the coming year; but keep in mind, everything may not come true.

The food served on Silvester depends on the family's preference. Many have a special Silvester punch recipe, or serve something sweet like "good luck cookies", which come in a variety of meaningful shapes:

1. The chimneysweeper – sweeps the bad spirits out of a house.

2. The pretzel – has crossed arms, and symbolizes the hope that a family will stay healthy and together.
3. The horseshoe – symbolizes the moon and its ability to break bad magic.

At midnight, we gather in the streets and wish our neighbors "Ein Gutes Neues Jahr". Right at midnight, the church bells ring everywhere and shortly after the fireworks start as well. There are public fireworks, but most of the fireworks are private. Some of them go on until the early morning hours, and there are so many that the towns, no matter how big or small, seem to be on fire.

Prost Neujahr!

Here is a soup my mother served when everybody came back from watching the fireworks:

Ochsenschwanzsuppe (Ox Tail Soup)

2 lb. ox tails
1 medium onion sliced
2 tbsp. vegetable oil
8 cups water
1 tsp. salt
4 peppercorns

¼ cup chopped fresh parsley
½ cup carrots diced
1 cup celery diced
1 bay leaf
1 – 15oz can diced tomatoes drained
1 tsp. dried thyme
1 tbsp. flour
1 tbsp. butter
¼ cup Madeira wine

- In a large Dutch oven, brown ox tails and onions in vegetable oil.
- Add water, salt, and peppercorns. Simmer uncovered for 2 hours.
- Cover and simmer for 3 additional hours.
- Add parsley, carrots, celery, bay leaf, tomatoes, and thyme.
- Simmer for an additional 30 minutes.
- Drain stock and refrigerate for 1 hour.
- Blend meat and vegetables in a food processor and reserve.
- Remove fat from top of stock and reheat.
- Brown flour in a large, dry, hot.
- Add butter and blend.
- A little at a time, add stock and vegetable/meat mixture, until all are combined.
- Taste to season.
- Add Madeira just before serving.

Silvester Bowle (New Year's Eve Punch)
Papa Schiel's Special Recipe

2 28oz. cans cut pineapple
6 tbsp. sugar
3 bottles carbonated water
5 bottles table wine medium sweet

- Mix pineapples (with juice) and sugar in a large punch bowl.
- Add the carbonated water and let stand for 15 minutes.
- Do not stir!
- Slowly add table wine and stir.
- Cool for about 8 hours.
- Before serving, taste to determine if the punch needs more sugar, the sweetness depends on the wine you choose.

Viel Glück Plätzchen (Good Luck Cookies)

2 cups all-purpose flour
3 tsp. baking powder
1 cup brown sugar
1 tsp. vanilla extract
1 tsp. cinnamon
¼ tsp. nutmeg
2 eggs
¾ cup butter cold and cut in cubes
⅓ cup ground hazelnuts
For the frosting:
1 cup confectioner's sugar
A few drops of lemon juice
2 egg whites
Food color if desired

- Preheat oven to 350° F and line cookie sheets with parchment paper.
- Mix flour and baking powder.
- Stir in sugar, spices, eggs, butter, and hazelnuts.
- Quickly knead to a smooth dough.
- If the dough is too dry, add an egg yolk; if the dough is too moist add a little more flour.
- Cool the dough in the refrigerator for 1 hour.

- On a floured surface, roll dough out until ¼-inch thick.
- Cut out horseshoes, pretzel, and chimneysweeper shapes.
- Put cookies on a cookie sheet and bake for 10 minutes, until golden brown.
- Let the cookies cool and decorate with the frosting.

At breakfast on January 1, "Neujahr", we serve little breads in the shape of a pig. Already in the middle ages the pig was a sign of affluence, and to this day it is a symbol of prosperity, wealth, fertility, and strength. We often give each other little pig figurines as a gift, with well wishes for the New Year.

Almost a must for lunch is Sauerkraut, Rippchen (smoked pork chops) and mashed potatoes. It is a salty meal and salt symbolizes money, which we all hope to have in the New Year.

Here Are Some More Typical German Recipes:

Salate (Salads)

Kartoffelsalat 1 (Potato Salad 1)

5 lb. small potatoes
4 hard-boiled eggs sliced
1 small onion chopped
3 tbsp. oil
3 tbsp. vinegar
1 tsp. salt
½ tsp. ground pepper
6 tbsp. mayonnaise
- Boil, and drain unpeeled potatoes the night before the salad is needed.
- The next day peel and slice potatoes.

- Add eggs, oil, vinegar, salt, and pepper and stir well.
- Stir in mayonnaise.
- Let the salad rest for about 3 hours in the refrigerator.
  Stir again before serving.

Kartoffelsalat 2 (Potato Salad 2)

The second potato salad is prepared just as the first one, but without the mayonnaise. Instead, fry and crumble eight slices of bacon, stir into the potato salad and serve right away.

Nudelsalat (Noodle Salad)

1 - 16oz. package small egg noodles cooked, drained and cooled
1 – 15oz. can peas and carrots drained
4 dill pickles chopped
1 lb. ring bologna in small cubes
5 hardboiled eggs, chopped
Seasoning:
1 tsp. salt
½ tsp. pepper
3 tbsp. oil
3 tbsp. vinegar
6 tbsp. mayonnaise

- Mix cooled noodles with peas, carrots, pickles, bologna, and eggs.
- Add seasonings and stir well.
- Chill salad for 3 hours.
- Stir and taste again before serving

Unser Familien Salat (Our Family Salad)

5 lb. small potatoes
1 lb. ring bologna
1 - 15oz. jar pickled red beets
1 - 15oz. jar pickled herring
4 dill pickles
Seasoning:
1 tsp. salt
½ tsp. pepper
3 tsp. sugar
6 tbsp. mayonnaise
8 tbsp. pickled beet juice

- Boil unpeeled potatoes the night before the salad is needed.
- Drain and let cool.
- The next day peel and slice potatoes.
- Put the bologna, red beets, herring, and pickles through a food processor with a medium grating disk.
- Mix potatoes with the grated ingredients.
- Add seasonings and stir carefully.
- Chill for about 6 hours or overnight, the longer the salad is chilled the better the flavor.
- Stir again before serving.
- Serve with French bread.

Wurstsalat (Meat Salad)

3 medium carrots
1 lb. sliced bologna
2 medium onions
3 dill pickles
1 small apple
1 tsp. sugar
1 tsp. soy sauce

1 tsp. pepper
2 tbsp. vinegar
4 tbsp. oil
6 tsp. chopped parsley

- Clean carrots and simmer in ½ cup of water for 10 minutes. Drain and let cool.
- Cut bologna in small stripes, the onion in fine rings, the carrots in stripes, and the apple and pickles in squares. Mix together.
- Mix sugar, soy sauce, pepper, vinegar, and oil.
- Pour over salad and stir well.
- Chill for 1 hour.
- Sprinkle chopped parsley over the salad.
- Serve with French bread and unsalted butter.

Herringssalat (Herring Salad)

8oz. pickled herring
½ green pepper seeded and diced
1 apple cored and diced
1 orange sectioned and diced
2 tsp. grated onion
2 tbsp. oil
1 tbsp. vinegar
4 lettuce leafs

- Combine all ingredients aside from the lettuce leafs.
- Chill for at least 1 hour.
- Serve on lettuce leafs.

Frühlingssalat (Spring Salad)

6 hardboiled eggs sliced1 lbs. fresh asparagus, cleaned, steamed, cooled, and cut in bite size pieces.

Marinade:
6 tbsp. mayonnaise
1 tsp. mustard
2 tbsp. sour cream
¼ tsp. pepper
¼ tsp. salt
1 tsp. sugar
2 tsp. chopped fresh parsley

- Carefully mix the marinade with the eggs and the asparagus.
- Serve with toast and unsalted butter.

Rindfleischsalat (Beef Salad)

2 lb. cooked beef cooled and cubed
1 large onion cut in rings
1 green pepper cubed
2 tomatoes cut in eights
2 pickles cubed
Marinade:
8oz. plain yoghurt
½ cup ketchup
1 tbsp. vinegar
¼ tsp. pepper
½ tsp. salt
¼ tsp. paprika
3 tbsp. fresh chopped parsley set aside

- Put meat and vegetables in a large bowl.
- Mix marinade and pour over salad.
- Stir well.
- Chill salad for at least 4 hours.
- Sprinkle parsley over salad before serving it.
- Serve with French bread.

Sauerkrautsalat (Cabbage Salad)

1 cup shredded radish
1 large apple shredded
1 – 15oz. can sauerkraut drained
Juice of a ½ lemon
½ cup sour cream
1 tsp. sugar
½ tsp. salt
¼ tsp. pepper
2 tbsp. fresh chives chopped
- Mix all ingredients well.
- Let the salad rest for 2 hours before serving.

Suppen (Soups)

Blumenkohlsuppe (Cauliflower Soup)

1 medium cauliflower
2 tbsp. flour
3 tbsp. butter
½ cup heavy cream
½ tsp. salt
¼ tsp. pepper
¾ tsp. nutmeg
4oz. ham cubed
4 cups water
- Clean and cut cauliflower.
- Cook in 4 cups of water until tender.
- Drain cauliflower and save cooking water.
- Blend cauliflower in a food processor.
- Melt butter in a large pot.
- Stir in flour quickly so no lumps remain.
- Add the cooking water and keep stirring.
- Add cauliflower, spices, heavy cream, and ham.

- If the soup is too thick for your liking, milk can be added.
- Stir well.
- Simmer for 5 minutes and serve.

Frankfurter Bohnensuppe (Frankfurter Bean Soup)

1 lbs. navy beans dried
8 cups water
3 cups beef broth
1 stalk of celery chopped
1 carrot chopped
2 small onions chopped
4 thick bacon strips cubed
1 tsp. salt
¼ tsp. pepper
6 Frankfurters (hot dogs) sliced
2 tbsp. parsley chopped
- Soak beans overnight.
- In a large saucepan, bring beans, water, and beef broth to a boil.
- Cook for 1 hour.
- Add carrot and celery and continue cooking for 30 minutes.
- In a separate frying pan, cook the bacon until crisp.
- Add the onions and cook until golden.
- Add bacon, onions, salt and pepper to soup.
- Add Frankfurters and heat for 5 minutes.
- Sprinkle soup with parsley and serve.

Griesssuppe (Grits Soup)
An emergency meal, for lean times

2½ tbsp. butter
4 tbsp. quick cooking grits
2 cups vegetable broth
¼ tsp. salt

¼ tsp. nutmeg
1 tbsp. parsley or chives (if available)
- In a medium pan, melt butter.
- Add grits and stir until golden brown.
- Stir in spices and vegetable broth and simmer for 15 minutes.
- Garnish with parsley or chives before serving.

Hessische Erdäpfelsuppe (Apple Soup from Hessen)

1 medium apple peeled and diced
2 medium potatoes cubed
3 thick slices bacon cubed
1 small onion diced
2 tbsp. oil
4 cups beef broth
1 cup fresh parsley chopped
½ tsp. salt
¼ tsp. pepper
1 cup plain small croutons
- Sauté potatoes, apple, bacon, and onion in vegetable oil.
- Add beef broth, salt, pepper, and parsley.
- Simmer for 25 minutes.
- Garnish with croutons before serving.

Karottenkremesuppe (Carrot Cream soup)

2 lb. fresh carrots
3 tbsp. butter
1 cup vegetable broth
½ cup heavy cream
½ tsp. salt
¼ tsp. pepper
1 tsp. lemon juice

2 tbsp. fresh parsley chopped
- Clean carrots and cut in 1-inch pieces.
- Melt butter in a large pot.
- Add carrots and stir for 5 minutes.
- Add vegetable broth and heavy cream.
- Simmer for 25 minutes.
- Blend carrots in a food processor.
- Return to pot, season with salt and pepper.
- Simmer for 10 minutes.
- Sprinkle chopped parsley over soup.
- Serve.

Krautsuppe (Cabbage Soup)

4 thick slices bacon cubed
2 onions chopped
2 carrots cubed
2 potatoes cubed
1 medium head green cabbage shredded
4 cubs chicken broth
2 cups water
6 sprigs parsley
1 bay leaf
½ tsp. salt
¼ tsp. pepper
- Tie parsley and bay leaf together with a string.
- Combine all ingredients, except salt and pepper, in a 6-quart pot.
- Partially cover and simmer for 2 hours.
- Discard the parsley/bay leaf bundle.
- Season soup with salt and pepper.
- Some families like to sprinkle Parmesan cheese over the soup.

Linsensuppe mit Frankfurter
(Lentil Soup with Frankfurter)

1 cup lentils dried (the quick cooking kind)
6 cups water
2 thick slices bacon cubed and cooked crisp
1 leek in thin rings
1 large carrot finely chopped
1 celery stalk finely chopped
1 onion finely chopped
1 tbsp. vegetable oil
2 tbsp. flour
1 tbsp. vinegar
4 Frankfurter Würstchen (hot dogs) sliced
1 tsp. salt
¼ tsp. pepper

- Wash lentils.
- In a 3-quart saucepan, bring 6 cups of water to a boil.
- Add lentils, bacon, leek, carrots, and celery.
- Simmer partially covered for 40 minutes.
- Meanwhile, sauté onion in vegetable oil until soft.
- Sprinkle flour over onions, stirring constantly.
- Add ½ cup of soup to the flour and onions and stir until well blended.
- Stir in vinegar.
- Add onion mixture to soup and stir well.
- Cover and simmer for 30 minutes, or until lentils are soft.
- Add Frankfurters, and simmer for 5 minutes.
- Season with salt and pepper.
- Serve.

Mehlsuppe (Flour Soup)
A very simple soup for true emergencies

5 tbsp. flour
4 tbsp. butter
1 onion chopped
4 cubs beef broth
½ cup grated cheese
- Cook flour in a dry, hot skillet until lightly brown.
- Add butter and mix well.
- Add onions and cook until softened, stirring constantly.
- Add broth, bring to a boil, and simmer for 20 minutes.
- Serve with grated cheese.

Ofen Nudelsuppe (Oven Noodle Soup)

2 tbsp. butter
2 cups cabbage shredded
2 cups carrots diced
1 leek in thin rings
9 oz. frozen peas
8 oz. medium shell noodles uncooked
8 cups chicken broth
16 sausage links cut in half
½ tsp. salt
½ tsp. pepper
- Mix cabbage, carrots, leek, peas, and noodles.
- Preheat oven to 350 degrees F.
- Butter a 6-quart Dutch oven (or other oven safe pot) and fill with vegetables and noodles.
- In a separate pot, bring broth to a boil.
- Add sausages to broth and cook 2 minutes.
- Pour broth over vegetables and noodles.
- Cover and cook in oven for 35 minutes.

Strohsuppe (Straw Soup)

2 cups potatoes peeled and cubed
1 – 15oz. can sauerkraut
2 small onions diced
4 thick slices bacon diced
2 tbsp. oil
6 cups vegetable broth
½ tsp. salt
¼ tsp. pepper

- Sauté onions and bacon in oil until golden brown.
- Add vegetable broth, sauerkraut, and potatoes.
- Bring to a boil, then simmer for 15 minutes.
- Add pepper and salt.
- Serve with thick slices of rye bread and unsalted butter.

Weinerntesuppe (Harvest Soup)

2 cups potatoes peeled and diced
1 small onion diced
1 leek in thin rings
2 tbsp. butter
4 cups beef broth
½ cup dry Riesling
1 bay leaf
¼ tsp. pepper
¼ tsp. salt
1 cup heavy cream
1 tsp. cornstarch mixed with ¼ cup cold water.

- In butter sauté potatoes, onions, and leek for 10 minutes.
- Do not brown.
- Add the Riesling and simmer for 5 minutes.
- Sir in the broth, salt, pepper, and bay leaf. Simmer for 20 minutes.

- Remove bay leaf.
- Add cream and stir well.
- Thicken soup with the cornstarch mixture. Bring to a boil, then immediately remove from heat.
- The soup is best served with fresh bread and a good glass of "Neroberg" or "Rhinehessen" Riesling.

Hauptgerichte (Main dishes)

Currywurst

4 Bratwurst fried or grilled
For the sauce:
1 – 15 oz. can tomato sauce
1 tsp. sugar
½ tsp. pepper
½ tsp. sweet paprika
2 tsp. curry powder
- Prepare 4 plates with ¼-inch slices of Bratwurst.
- Mix all ingredients for the sauce well.
- Pour 2 tbsp. of sauce over each Bratwurst.
- Serve with Brötchen or French bread.

Deutsche Pfanne (German Casserole)

12 oz. spaghetti cooked
1 – 15 oz. can sauerkraut drained
1 lb. ground beef
1 medium egg beaten
½ cup breadcrumbs
¼ cup milk
1 tsp. salt
½ tsp. sugar
½ tsp. pepper
1 tbsp. olive oil

2 – 15 oz. cans diced tomatoes
- Preheat oven to 350° F.
- Mix together spaghetti and sauerkraut.
- In another bowl, mix beef, breadcrumbs, egg, salt sugar, and pepper.
- Form 20 meatballs.
- Sauté meatballs in olive oil until browned.
- Add tomatoes and simmer for 10 minutes.
- Place half the noodle mix in a 13x9 inch baking dish.
- Add half the meatballs, then the remaining noodle mixture, and top with meatballs.
- Bake for 1 hour at 350 degrees F.

Hasenpfeffer (Rabbit Pepper)

1 cleaned rabbit cut into 8 pieces
2 tbsp. vegetable oil
1 bay leaf crumbled
1 tsp. minced garlic
1 whole glove
2 thick slices bacon diced
2 medium carrots chopped
½ cup vinegar
1½ cup water
1 cup sour cream
- Heat vegetable oil in a saucepan.
- Add bay leaf, garlic, whole glove, bacon, and carrots to the hot oil.
- Stir a few times, add rabbit pieces, and brown on all sides.
- Mix vinegar and water and pour over meat.
- Bring to a boil.
- Cover and simmer for 2 hours until meat is tender.
- Add sour cream before removing from heat.
- Serve with dumplings or noodles.

Kalbsgulasch (Veal Goulash)

3 lb. breast of boned veal cut in large cubes
2 medium onions finely chopped
3 tbsp. vegetable oil
2 tomatoes peeled and chopped
1 cup water
1 tsp. salt
1 tsp. pepper
½ tsp. sweet paprika
3 tbsp. flour
¼ cup water

- Brown meat and onions in a large saucepan.
- Add tomatoes, salt, pepper, and paprika.
- Bring to a boil.
- Cover and simmer for 1½ hour.
- Stir frequently.
- Mix flour with ¼ cup water until smooth.
- Add enough to the goulash to thicken the gravy.
- Taste to see if salt or pepper is needed.
- Serve with dumplings.

Kalbshaxe (Veal Shank)

1 large (3-4 lbs.) veal shank
6 medium carrots chopped
2 onions chopped
2 stalks of celery chopped
1¼ tsp. salt
1 tsp. pepper
1 tbsp. vinegar
Water as needed
3 tbsp. butter

- Cook vegetables in a large pot, with just enough water to cover them, for 15 minutes.

- When cooked, add veal shank, spices, and vinegar, and simmer for 3 hours.
- Check the dish about every 30 minutes; adding more water when necessary.
- Remove veal shank and brown in hot butter until crisp.
- Serve with potato salad.

The vegetables and the vegetable water provide a fine base for a soup. So keep it for another meal.

Königsberger Klopse (Königsberger Meatballs)

1 lb. ground chuck
1 lb. ground pork
1 medium onion grated
⅓ cup bread crumbs
½ tsp. salt
½ tsp. pepper
¼ tsp. nutmeg
5 egg whites beaten stiff
Sauce:
3 cups water
1 medium onion chopped
4 bay leaves
1 tbsp. sugar
1 tsp. salt
¼ tsp. allspice
¼ tsp. peppercorns
¼ cup vinegar
1 tbsp. flour
5 egg yolks beaten
1 tbsp. capers

- Combine all ingredients for the meatballs, adding egg whites last
- Form into 1½-inch size meatballs.

- In a large saucepan, bring water, chopped onion, bay leaves, sugar, salt, allspice, and peppercorns to a boil.
- Boil for 30 minutes, strain, and return liquid to pot.
- Bring to a boil again, add meatballs, and simmer 15 minutes.
- Remove meatballs.
- Add vinegar to liquid.
- Stir flour into a small amount of cold water. Combine with beaten egg yolks.
- Add the mixture gradually to the liquid, stirring until smooth and thick.
- Pour sauce over meatballs, garnish with capers, and serve over rice.

Leberklösschen (Liver Dumplings)

½ lb. calf's liver
3 small hard rolls
1 cup water
1 onion chopped
2 tbsp. fresh parsley chopped
2 tbsp. flour
2 large eggs
1 tsp. salt
½ tsp. nutmeg
½ tsp. marjoram
2 quarts beef stock

- Grind liver.
- Break up rolls and soak in water for 5 minutes.
- Squeeze excess water from rolls.
- Mix liver, rolls, onion, parsley, and spices.
- Form 2-inch balls.
- Bring beef stock to a boil, drop balls into stock and cook for 10 minutes.
- Serve with Sauerkraut and mashed potatoes.

Pilze in Sahnesosse
(Mushrooms in Cream Sauce)

2 lb. fresh mushrooms
4 slices thick bacon diced
4 tbsp. butter
1 cup white wine
½ tsp. salt
¼ tsp. pepper
¼ tsp. paprika
Pinch nutmeg
1 cup heavy cream
Juice of ½ lemon
2 tbsp. fresh parsley chopped

- Clean mushrooms and slice in half. Pat dry.
- Fry bacon in large pan until lightly browned.
- Remove from pan and reserve.
- Add butter to the pan drippings.
- Add onion and sauté until lightly browned.
- Add mushrooms, cook until tender, stirring often.
- Stir in wine and spices.
- Cover pan and simmer over low heat for 15 minutes.
- Remove from heat. Add the bacon, cream, and lemon juice.
- Reheat until just warm. Do not boil.
- Garnish with parsley.
- Serve over egg noodles.

Rehschmortopf (Venison Casserole)

3 lb. venison cubed
4 thick slices bacon diced
2 tbsp. flour
2 cups beef broth
½ cup red wine
½ cup red wine vinegar

1 tsp. salt
½ tsp. pepper
1 medium bay leaf crushed
1 glove garlic chopped
2 tbsp. fresh parsley chopped
½ tsp. thyme
2 large onions chopped
1 cup fresh mushrooms sliced
1 tsp. cornstarch mixed with 2 tbsp. cold water

- Sauté onions and cook bacon until crisp. Remove from pan.
- Add venison to bacon fat and brown all over.
- Sprinkle with flour on venison and stir.
- Add broth, wine, and vinegar, stir.
- Add salt, pepper, bay leaf, garlic, parsley, thyme, crumbled bacon and onions.
- Simmer for 1 hour.
- Add mushrooms and simmer for 20 minutes.
- Stir in cornstarch mixture and simmer until sauce is thickened.
- Serve over noodles or rice.

Rindergulasch (Beef Goulash)

1 lb. beef chuck cubed
2 medium onions chopped
3 tbsp. butter
1 tsp. salt
½ tsp. pepper
½ tsp. paprika
2 cups water
2 tbsp. flour
3 cups beef stock
1 tsp. cornstarch mixed with 2 tbsp. cold water

- Brown onions in butter.
- Add meat and fry until browned.

- Add water and spices.
- Cover and simmer for 1 hour.
- When liquid has evaporated, sprinkle with flour and brown the flour lightly.
- Add beef stock and simmer for 30 minutes.
- Add cornstarch mixture and simmer until sauce is thickened.
- Serve over spätzle or dumplings.

Rippenspeer (Ribs of Pork)

3 lb. smoked pork rib roast
1 onion chopped
1 tomato chopped
1 celery chopped
1 tbsp. butter
1 cup water
1 tbsp. flour
½ cup water
½ cup sour cream
1 tsp. salt
½ tsp. pepper

- Preheat oven to 350° F.
- Wash and dry meat, set in roasting pan, and sprinkle with salt and pepper.
- Spread butter, onion and tomato on top. Add 1 cup of water.
- Cover with foil and steam in oven for 1 hour until water has evaporated.
- Remove pan from oven and put it on top of the stove over medium heat.
- Remove foil and brown the meat in the pan on all sides.
- Remove meat and keep it hot.
- Add flour and water to the pan to make the gravy, stirring well.

- Add cream and additional seasoning if desired.
- Serve with red potatoes sprinkled with fresh parsley.

Rostbraten mit Pilzfüllung
(Roast with Mushroom Stuffing)

2 lb. flank steak
½ tsp. salt
¼ tsp. pepper
1 tsp. Dijon mustard
For the mushroom stuffing:
2 tbsp. vegetable oil
1 small onion chopped
4 oz. fresh mushrooms chopped
½ cup fresh parsley chopped
2 tbsp. fresh chives chopped
1 tbsp. tomato paste
½ cup dried breadcrumbs
¼ tsp. salt
¼ tsp. pepper
1 tsp. paprika
For the gravy:
3 thick slices bacon cubed
2 small onions chopped
1 cup hot beef broth
1 tsp. Dijon mustard
1 tbsp. tomato paste

- Salt and pepper flank steak.
- Spread one side with mustard.
- To prepare the stuffing, heat vegetable oil in frying pan.
- Add onion and cook for 3 minutes until lightly brown,
- Add mushrooms and cook for 5 minutes.
- Stir in parsley, chives, tomato paste, breadcrumbs, salt, pepper, and paprika.

- Spread stuffing on mustard side of steak. Roll up and tie with string.
- Cook bacon in a Dutch oven until partially done.
- Add the meat roll and brown on all sides, for 10 minutes.
- Add onions and sauté for 5 minutes.
- Add beef broth, cover, and simmer for 1 hour.
- Remove meat.
- Season pan juices with mustard, salt and pepper, and tomato paste.
- If needed the gravy can be thickened by adding 1 tbsp. cornstarch mixed in 2 tbsp. cold water.
- Serve with dumplings.

Rindfleischrouladen (Beef Rolls)

8 (4oz. each) cube steaks pounded very thin
¼ cup yellow mustard
2 tsp. salt
2 tsp. pepper
16 thin slices bacon
3 tbsp. vegetable oil
1 (12oz.) can beef broth
1½ cups water
2 tbsp. cornstarch
1 cup cold water
¼ cup sour cream

- Spread ½ tbsp. mustard over one side of each piece of meat.
- Sprinkle salt and pepper evenly over the steaks.
- Place 2 slices of bacon on each steak.
- Roll up each steak and secure with toothpicks.
- Heat the oil in a skillet over a medium heat.
- Cook meat on all sides until browned.
- Add beef broth and water and bring to a boil.

- Reduce heat and simmer for about 45 minutes until tender.
- Remove meat rolls.
- Whisk together cornstarch and cold water. Stir into skillet for 3 minutes until sauce is thickened.
- Stir in sour cream.
- Serve with butter noodles.

Sauerbraten (Sour Roast)

4 lb. beef rump or sirloin tip
For the marinade:
1½ cups vinegar (I prefer Heinz white vinegar)
1 cup water
1 medium onion in rings
3 whole bay leaves
10 whole peppercorns
½ tsp. mustard seeds
For cooking the Sauerbraten:
3 tbsp. oil
1 cup hot beef broth
3 tbsp. gingerbread crumbs
3 tbsp. flour
4 tbsp. heavy cream
3 tbsp. raisins

- 3 days before needed, clean meat and place in a large zip lock bag.
- Mix marinade, pour over meat, seal bag tightly, and lay flat in a 9x13 inch pan.
- Place in the refrigerator and turn meat twice a day.
- When ready to cook, remove meat and dry well.
- Strain marinade and set it aside.
- Heat oil in a Dutch oven, and brown meat from both sides.
- Add beef broth and 5 tbsp. of the marinade.
- Cover and simmer on low heat for 80 minutes.

- About ½-inch of liquid should be in the Dutch oven at all times, so add more liquid during cooking time if needed.
- Add gingerbread crumbs and simmer for another 10 minutes.
- Set meat aside.
- Strain gravy, return to Dutch oven, add marinade, and bring to a boil.
- Mix flour and heavy cream and add to gravy. Reduce heat, and simmer for 5 minutes.
- Add raisins.
- Slice meat and serve with gravy, red cabbage, applesauce, and potato dumplings.

Schusterpfanne (Shoemakers Pot)

2 lb. pork loin roast
1 tsp. salt
¼ tsp. pepper
12 small red potatoes cut in half
3 green ripe pears, peeled and cut into eights
¼ tsp. marjoram
¼ tsp. dill weed seed
1 tbsp. caraway seed
1 tbsp. beef broth granules
2 cups boiling water
2 tbsp. cornstarch
¼ cup cold water

- Sprinkle pork with salt and pepper. Place in Dutch oven.
- Arrange potatoes and pears around meat.
- Sprinkle marjoram, dill, and caraway seeds over meat, potatoes, and pears.
- Mix beef broth and boiling water, pour into Dutch oven. Cover.

- Bring to a boil, then reduce heat and simmer for 1½ hours or until meat is tender when pierced with a fork.
- Remove meat, potatoes and pears and place on a platter.
- Mix cornstarch with cold water and stir into Dutch oven.
- Simmer, stirring constantly, until sauce is thickened.
- Serve with a glass of Riesling and fresh bread with butter.

Schweinefilet (Pork Tenderloins)

1 lb. pork tenderloin
½ tsp. salt
¼ tsp. pepper
1 onion sliced
1 tomato chopped
2 tbsp. butter
¼ cup beef broth
1 tbsp. flour
2 tbsp. water
1 tbsp. sour cream
¼ cup white wine

- Slice pork into ¾-inch thick fillets.
- Melt butter in a large frying pan.
- Fry filets over high heat on both sides.
- Add onion rings, tomato, and beef broth.
- Bring to a boil. Reduce heat and simmer for 25 minutes.
- Remove meat.
- Strain beef broth and return to pan.
- Mix flour with water and add to beef broth stirring constantly.
- Add sour cream and white wine.

- Pour gravy over fillets and serve with buttered noodles.

Schnitzel (Veal Cutlet)

4 veal steaks cut ½-inch thick (boneless pork steaks or chops can be used instead)
½ tsp. salt
½ tsp. pepper
3 tbsp. flour
1 egg
4 tbsp. milk
1 cup breadcrumbs
3 tbsp. oil
4 slices lemon
- Sprinkle veal steaks with salt and pepper.
- Beat egg and mix with the milk.
- Dip both sides of steaks in flour, then into the milk mixture, and finally into the breadcrumbs.
- Let steaks rest for five minutes.
- Heat oil in frying pan and fry steaks on each side for four minutes, until breadcrumbs are crisp and brown. (Pork chops need about seven minutes on each side.)
- Garnish each Schnitzel with a slice of lemon.

Here are two delicious variations for Schnitzel:

Jägerschnitzel (Hunters Veal Cutlet)

The cutlets are prepared per the recipe above.
For the sauce:
1 cup fresh mushrooms sliced
1 small onion chopped
½ cup boiling beef broth

¼ cup heavy cream

2 tbsp. cornstarch

3 tbsp. cold water

- Sauté onions and mushrooms for 5 minutes in the meat juice left in the pan.
- Add boiling broth and bring to a simmer.
- Mix cornstarch with cold water.
- Stir heavy cream into sauce.
- A little at a time, add the cornstarch mixture until sauce is thickened.
- Serve sauce over Schnitzel with French fries or croquette.

Zigeuner Schnitzel (Gypsy Veal Cutlet)

Prepare cutlets are as above.

For the sauce:

1 tbsp. butter

1 cup of mushrooms

1 small onion halved and sliced

1 green bell pepper cut in 1-inch stripes

1 red bell pepper cut in 1-inch stripes

¼ cup flour

1 medium dill pickle cut in 1-inch stripes

1 ½ cups beef broth

- Add butter to the meat juice left in pan.
- Add mushrooms, onion, and bell peppers and sauté until tender.
- Sprinkle with flour and stir to blend.
- Add beef broth. Continue to cook until sauce is thickened.
- Add the pickle.
- Taste and add salt if needed.
- Serve over cutlet with French fries.

Nachtische (Desserts)

Kaffeecreme (Coffee Cream)

½ cup double-strength coffee
½ cup heavy cream
2½ tbsp. sugar
2 tbsp. cornstarch
1 egg, separated
3 tbsp. Water
Chocolate shavings

- Beat egg white until very stiff.
- Add cream, and sugar to the coffee and bring to a boil.
- Mix cornstarch with 3 tbsp. water, stir into mixture, and cook for 3 minutes, stirring constantly.
- Remove from heat.
- Stir in egg yolk and bring back to a boil.
- Remove from heat.
- Fold in beaten egg white, pour into glass bowl, and chill thoroughly.
- Decorate with chocolate shavings before serving.

Mandelflammeri (Almond Pudding)

2 tbsp. cornstarch
1 cup milk
2 tbsp. sugar
Pinch of salt
1 tbsp. finely chopped almonds
1 tbsp. butter
1 egg, separated

- Stir cornstarch into 3 tbsp. of milk.
- Bring the rest of the milk, sugar, salt, and almonds to a boil.

- Add cornstarch mixture and let cook for 3 minutes, stirring constantly.
- Remove from heat and stir in butter and egg yolk.
- Fold in beaten egg white.
- Rinse out a glass dish with cold water and, while still moist, pour in pudding and chill.

Semmelauflauf (Almond Soufflés)

6 hard rolls
1 cup milk
5 tbsp. butter
1 cup sugar
3 eggs, separated
Zest and juice of ½ lemon
1 cup almonds finely chopped
½ cup raisins
Good vanilla ice cream
- Preheat oven to 425° F.
- Slice rolls and soak in milk until milk is absorbed.
- Beat egg whites until very stiff.
- Cream butter. Stir in sugar, egg yolks, lemon zest, and juice.
- Fold almonds, raisins, soaked rolls, and beaten egg whites into the butter mixture.
- Bake in a greased baking dish for 30 minutes.
- Serve warm with ice cream.

Schokoladencreme (Chocolate Cream)

1 egg yolk
2 tbsp. sugar
1½ oz. milk chocolate grated
3 tbsp. very strong coffee
1 cup heavy cream, whipped

2 tbsp. chocolate shavings
- Stir egg yolk and sugar until foamy.
- Melt chocolate in a double boiler.
- Stir in coffee and combine with egg yolk mixture.
- Beat thoroughly.
- Fold in whipped cream.
- Pour into glass dish and chill.
- Sprinkle with chocolate shavings before serving.

Vanillecreme (Vanilla Cream)

2 packages unflavored gelatin
½ cup cold water
9 tbsp. sugar
1 tbsp. cornstarch
2 large eggs, beaten
1½ cups scalded milk
1   cup good vanilla ice cream
1 tsp. vanilla
1 cup heavy cream, whipped
- Sprinkle gelatin over cold water to soften and heat to dissolve gelatin completely.
- Mix sugar and cornstarch. Add eggs and beat for 2 minutes.
- Slowly add warm milk, beating constantly.
- Pour into a 1-quart saucepan.
- Cook over medium heat until custard coats a spoon.
- While custard is hot, add gelatin and ice cream.
- Cool until slightly thickened.
- Add vanilla.
- Fold in whipped cream.
- Pour into a 1-quart mold or glass dish, chill until set.
- Carefully remove from mold.
- Cream can be served with a garnish of seasonal fresh fruits.

Weincreme (Wine Cream)

2 cups sherry or white wine
1 cup water
½ cup sugar
5 eggs
Zest and juice of ½ lemon
Seedless grapes for garnish
- Stir all ingredients until thick and foamy in a double boiler over a low heat.
- Pour into sherbet glasses and chill.
- Garnish with grapes before serving.

Zwetschgenknödel (Plum Dumplings)

3 lb. potatoes
5 cups flour
4 tbsp. sugar
2 eggs beaten
Pinch of salt
4 tbsp. butter, melted
2 lb. plums
Cubes of sugar
½ cup breadcrumbs
8 tbsp. butter
Cinnamon and sugar
- Cook, peel, and mash potatoes.
- Turn out onto a floured breadboard.
- Add flour, sugar, eggs, salt and 4 tbsp. melted butter and mix to form a firm dough.
- Roll to ½ inch thick and cut into pieces the size of your palm.
- Remove pits from plums and replace them with sugar cubes.
- Place one plum on each slice of dough.
- Fold dough around plums to cover completely.

- Cook in water 5 to 8 minutes.
- Melt 8 tbsp. butter and stir in breadcrumbs.
- Roll finished dumplings in breadcrumb and butter mix and sprinkle with cinnamon and sugar.

Kuchen und Torten (Cakes and Tortes)

Apfeltorte (Apple Torte)

2 eggs
1 cup vegetable oil
2 cups sugar
2 tsp. ground cinnamon
½ tsp. salt
1 tsp. vanilla extract
2 cups all-purpose flour
1 tsp. baking soda
4 cups apples, peeled, cored and diced
1 pint whipping cream
½ cup confectioner's sugar

- Preheat oven to 350° F.
- Grease and flour a spring-form pan.
- Beat oil and eggs with an electric mixer until creamy. Add sugar and vanilla and blend well.
- Combine flour, salt, baking soda, and cinnamon together in a bowl. Slowly add to the egg mixture and mix well until batter is thick.
- Fold in the apples with a wooden spoon. Spread batter into a prepared pan.
- Bake for 45 minutes or until toothpick comes out clean.
- Let the cake cool and dust with ¼ cup confectioner's sugar.
- Whip the cream with the rest of the confectioner's sugar until stiff.
- Cut cake in 12 slices and serve with whipped cream.

Butterkuchen (Butter Cake)

2 packages active dry yeast
½ cup lukewarm water
¾ cup milk
½ cup sugar
1 tsp. salt
½ cup butter
4 cups all-purpose flour
Grated zest of 1 lemon
3 eggs
For the butter topping:
½ cup cold butter
1 cup sugar
½ tsp. cinnamon
⅓ cup almonds, blanched, and slivered

- Sprinkle the yeast over warm water.
- Heat milk, sugar, salt and ½ cup butter until butter is melted.
- Cool milk mixture to lukewarm, and then add dissolved yeast.
- Place the flour, mixed with the lemon rind, in a large bowl. Form a well in the center.
- Add the yeast-milk mixture and eggs. Stir until blended and smooth.
- Pour into a buttered 9x13 inch baking pan, spreading dough evenly.
- Let rise in a warm place for about 45 minutes.
- Preheat oven to 375° F.
- Mix the cold butter, sugar, and cinnamon, until fine particles form.
- Sprinkle over cake.
- Sprinkle almonds on top.
- Bake for 30 minutes until top is golden brown.
- Cool and serve.

Donauwellen (Danube Waves)

1⅛ cups butter, softened
1 cup sugar
5 eggs
1 tsp. vanilla extract
3 cups all-purpose flour
1 tsp. salt
1 tbsp. baking soda
¼ cup unsweetened cocoa powder
1 tbsp. milk
3 cups canned pitted sour cherries, drained
For the topping:
3 tbsp. cornstarch
½ cup sugar
1½ tsp. vanilla extract
7 oz. semisweet chocolate, shaved

- Preheat oven to 350° F. Grease a 9x13 inch baking pan.
- Cream the butter with 1 cup of sugar in an electric mixer.
- Mix in the eggs one at a time, then stir in vanilla.
- Combine flour, salt, and baking soda,
- Fold into the egg mixture.
- Spread ⅔ of the batter into the prepared baking dish.
- Stir cocoa powder and 1 tbsp. milk into the remaining batter until blended. Spread evenly over vanilla layer.
- Pat cherries dry with a paper towel and sprinkle over batter.
- Bake 40 to 50 minutes until toothpick comes out clean. Let cool.
- For the topping, mix together the cornstarch, sugar, and 3 tbsp. of milk.
- Heat remaining milk in a saucepan just until hot but not boiling.

- Stir in the cornstarch mixture and remove from the heat. Cool for 5 minutes stirring constantly.
- Stir in vanilla. Let mixture cool completely, then spread over cooled cake.
- Sprinkle shaved chocolate on to the cake. Chill for about 5 hours before serving.

Drei Königs Kuchen (Three Kings Cake)
Served in many areas on January 6· It symbolizes a king's crown.

2 cups all-purpose flour
3 tbsp. all-purpose flour
1.4 oz. fresh yeast (can be found at any large grocery store by the cream cheese)
¼ cup lukewarm milk
1 tbsp. lukewarm milk
7 tbsp. butter, melted
½ tsp. salt
1 tsp. vanilla extract
½ tsp. cardamom
2 eggs
½ cup raisins soaked in 2 tbsp. Rum
1 cup chopped mixed dry fruit (apricot, cherries, etc.)
1 beaten egg yolk
For the frosting:
6 tbsp. Confectioner's sugar
2 tbsp. lemon juice
½ cup red candied cherries, halved.

- Preheat oven to 350° F and grease a spring-form pan.
- Put ¾ of the flour into a large bowl. Create a well in the middle, crumble in the yeast. Mix with a pinch of sugar and some of the lukewarm milk. Sprinkle a little flour on top.
- Cover with a cloth and let rise in a warm place for 15 minutes.

- Add the melted butter, salt, lemon, cardamom, eggs, remaining milk, and flour to the yeast mixture. Knead until dough is smooth.
- When the dough begins to form a ball, stir in raisins and dry fruit.
- Form dough into a log. Cut the log into 4 small pieces of dough, and 4 large pieces. Roll each piece into a ball.
- Set the balls alternating around the outside of the spring-form pan. Cover the pan with a cloth and let it rise in a warm place for 15 minutes.
- Uncover pan and brush dough with beaten egg yolk.
- Bake cake for about 30 minutes until golden brown.
- Let cool and remove from pan.
- Mix lemon juice and confectioner's sugar to an icing consistency (not to thin). Spread over cake and garnish with candied cherries.

Frankfurter Kranz (Frankfurter Wreath)

For the cake batter:
6 eggs
½ cup lukewarm water
1¾ cups sugar
2¾ cups all-purpose flour
2 tsp. baking powder
8 tbsp. butter melted and cooled
For the butter cream:
1 package vanilla pudding
½ cup sugar
2 cups cold milk
16 tbsp. butter at room temperature
For the Krokant (topping):
1 tsp. butter
1 tbsp. sugar
4 oz. chopped almonds

Additional ingredients:
1 jar red currant jelly
Candied cherries

- Preheat oven to 350° F and grease a spring-form pan with a central tube.
- For the batter, beat eggs and water together until the mixture doubles in volume.
- Gradually add sugar.
- Mix flour and baking powder together, sift over egg mixture, and then fold it in gently with a spatula.
- Fold in the melted and cooled butter.
- Pour batter into prepared spring-form pan and bake for about 40 minutes until a toothpick comes out clean. Set aside and cool.
- For the butter-cream, mix the vanilla pudding and sugar.
- Heat the milk in a pot, bring it to a boil, and then remove it from the heat.
- Add the vanilla mixture, whisking quickly until combined.
- Set pudding aside and allow it to cool to room temperature.
- Whip the butter in a mixer until it becomes fluffy. Fold in the cooled pudding a little at a time. Continue until all the pudding and butter is combined and the butter-cream is smooth.
- For the Krokant, mix all ingredients in a pan. Heat until almonds become slightly browned, transfer on a lined parchment paper sheet to cool.
- Cut the cake into three even layers.
- Place the bottom layer on a cake plate and cover it with a thin layer of jelly. Add a thin layer of butter-cream on top of the jelly.
- Now place the middle layer of cake on the butter-cream, spread a thin layer of jelly on this layer, followed by a layer of butter-cream. Top this with the last layer of cake.

- Frost the outside of the cake with the rest of the butter- cream, reserving about 6 tablespoons for decoration.
- Sprinkle the Krokant on the cream and press it on slightly.
- Place the rest of the butter-cream into a piping bag with a decorative tip. Create miniature mounds of cream on top of the cake spread evenly.
- Put one candied cherry on top of each mound.
- Chill in refrigerator for 3 hours before cutting and serving.

Gugelhupf (Bundt Cake)

1 package active dry yeast
1 cup milk, scalded and cooled
1 cup sugar
1 cup butter at room temperature
5 large eggs
1 tsp. vanilla extract
1 tbsp. lemon zest
¾ cup raisins
⅓ cup ground almonds
½ tsp. salt
4 cups all-purpose flour, unsifted
½ cup confectioner's sugar, for dusting.

- Sprinkle yeast into milk to dissolve.
- In a large bowl, beat sugar and butter until light and fluffy.
- Beat in eggs one at a time.
- Stir in vanilla, lemon rind, raisins, and almonds.
- Mix salt with flour and combine with the milk mixture.
- Grease a Bundt-cake pan, or a spring-form pan with a central tube.

- Pour batter into pan, cover, and let rise in a warm place until doubled, about 2 hours.
- Preheat oven to 375° F.
- Bake Gugelhupf for 40 minutes until browned and toothpick comes out clean.
- Remove from pan and it cool completely.
- Dust with confectioner's sugar.

Marmorkuchen (Marble Cake)

1 cup butter
1¾ cups sugar
5 egg yolks
3½ cups all-purpose flour
1 cup milk
1 tsp. vanilla extract
2 tsp. baking powder
5 egg whites, beaten stiff
2 tbsp. unsweetened cocoa
3 tbsp. sugar
½ cup confectioner's sugar for dusting

- Preheat oven to 350° F and grease a Bundt-cake pan, or a spring-form pan with a central tube.
- Cream butter, vanilla, and the sugar until fluffy.
- Beat in egg yolks and continue beating for 10 minutes.
- Gradually alternate stirring in flour, and milk until well combined.
- Stir in baking powder.
- Fold beaten egg whites into the batter.
- Reserve ⅓ of the batter and pour the rest into prepared pan.
- Mix cocoa and 3 tbsp. sugar with the reserved batter.
- Pour onto batter in pan.

- Bake for 60 to 70 minutes until slightly browned and a toothpick comes out clean.
- Let cake rest in the pan for 10 minutes, then turn it onto a wire rack and let it cool completely. Dust with confectioner's sugar.

Schwarzwälder Kirschtort
(Black Forest Torte)

For the cake:
6 egg yolks
3 tbsp. warm water
1 cup sugar
1 tsp. vanilla extract
6 egg whites, beaten stiff
1¼ cups all-purpose flour
¼ cup cornstarch
3 tsp. baking powder
½ cup unsweetened cocoa powder
2 tbsp. unsweetened cocoa powder
For filling #1:
8 oz. canned sour cherries, drained (save 1 cup of juice).
¼ cup sugar
Pinch of cinnamon
2 tsp. cornstarch
3 tbsp. cold water
For filling #2:
1 pint heavy whipping cream
¼ cup sugar
2 packages whip-it (a whipping cream stabilizer that can be found in the international food section at the grocery store)
2 tbsp. Kirschwasser (Schnapps)
1 tbsp. water
For cake decoration:

1 cup heavy whipping cream
1 package whip-it
2 tsp. confectioner's sugar
16 fresh or canned cherries
Chocolate shreds

- Preheat oven to 375° F and grease a spring-form pan.
- For the cake, beat egg yolks with the water and add vanilla and sugar.
- Keep beating until egg yolks have doubled in volume.
- Fold stiff egg whites into egg yolks with a spatula.
- Sift together flour, cornstarch, cocoa powder, and baking powder.
- Fold the flour mixture to the egg mixtures until combined.
- Fill a spring-form pan with batter and bake for 25 minutes or until toothpick comes out clean.
- Remove cake from oven and allow to cool completely.
- To make filling #1, combine sugar, cinnamon, and 1 cup of cherry juice. Bring to a boil, then remove from heat.
- Mix cornstarch with the water.
- Whisk cornstarch into cherry juice and return to a boil, continue whisking so no clumps form.
- Add cherries and allow mixture to boil for another minute.
- Remove from heat and cool completely.
- To make filling #2 whip cream, Whip-it it, and sugar until stiff peaks form.
- To finish the cake, slice it into 3 even layers.
- Place the bottom layer into a clean spring form pan or cake ring.

- Spread a thin layer of filling #2 on the bottom layer. Top it with filling #1.
- Put the next layer of cake on top and press down slightly. Drizzle the 2-tablespoon of Kirschwasser on this layer.
- Top this layer with the rest of filling #2.
- Top with the third layer of cake pressing down slightly.
- Put the cake in the refrigerator over-night for firmness.
- The next day, beat the whipping cream, whip-it, and confectioner's sugar until stiff peaks form.
- Gently remove the spring-form or cake ring from cake.
- Spread ⅔ of the cream on top and the sides of the cake.
- Decorate the cake by creating mounds from the remaining cream. Sprinkle chocolate shavings on top and the sides of the cake. Set 16 cherries along the top edge of the cake.
- Store cake in the refrigerator.

Streuselkuchen (Crumb Cake)

For the cake:
2¼ cups all-purpose flour
¼ cup sugar
¼ tsp. salt
1 package active dry yeast
¾ cup milk
½ cup butter
1 large egg
For the topping:
½ cup sugar
2 tsp. cinnamon

1 cup all-purpose flour

½ cup cold butter

- Preheat oven to 350° F. Grease and flour a 9x9 inch cake pan.
- To make the cake mix 1 cup of flour, sugar, salt and yeast in a large bowl.
- Heat milk and butter in a saucepan until very warm (about 130°F).
- Gradually add heated milk and butter mixture mixture to the dry ingredients. Beat for 2 minutes.
- Beat in 1 egg and 1 cup of flour for 2 minutes.
- Stir in the rest of the flour until the batter is soft but stiff.
- Spread batter into prepared cake pan.
- For the topping, mix all the dry ingredients, then cut in the butter until the mixture crumbles.
- Sprinkle this topping over batter.
- Cover with a cloth and let rise in a warm place until for about 2 hours until it doubles in size.
- Bake the cake for about 45 minutes or until toothpick comes out clean.

Weintraubentorte (Grape Torte)

2 cups all-purpose flour

⅔ cup sugar

¼ cup butter

1 egg 1 egg yolk

Grated zest of 1 lemon

⅛ tsp. salt

1 lb. seedless grapes (red or green)

3 egg whites

6 tbsp. sugar

Juice of ½ lemon

4 oz. ground almonds

- Sift flour and sugar into a medium size bowl.

- Cut in butter until mixture resembles coarse crumbs.
- Add egg, egg yolk, lemon rind, and salt. Mix with a fork to form a dough.
- Cover dough and let rest in the refrigerator for 20 minutes.
- Preheat oven to 350° F.
- Roll out dough into a circle, place on the bottom of an ungreased spring-form pan. Form a 1-inch high rim.
- Bake for 10 minutes.
- In the meantime, clean and half grapes.
- Beat egg whites until stiff, blend in lemon juice, sugar, and ground almonds.
- Carefully fold in the grapes.
- Remove the cake from the oven, and fill with the grape mixture.
- Return it to the oven and bake for 30 minutes. The filling should be slightly golden.
- Remove the cake from oven and let rest it for 10 minutes.
- Slowly remove the cake from the spring-form pan and let it cool completely on a wire rack.

Zitronenkuchen (Lemon Cake)

1⅛ cups butter, softened
1¼ cups sugar
5 eggs
2 tsp. vanilla extract
1 cup all-purpose flour
1 cup cornstarch
⅓ cup lemon juice
1 cup confectioner's sugar

- Preheat oven to 350° F. Grease a 9x5 inch loaf pan.
- In a large bowl beat butter and sugar together until light and fluffy.
- Beat in the eggs, one at a time.

- Stir in the vanilla, then mix in the flour and cornstarch.
- Pour into the prepared loaf pan.
- Bake for 1 hour and 15 minutes until a toothpick inserted to the crown comes out clean.
- Cool for 10 minutes before removing from the pan.
- Meanwhile, mix the lemon juice with the confectioner's sugar.
- Remove the cake from the pan and poke with a knitting needle (or something similar) all over.
- Pour glace over the top and let it soak in.
- Let cake cool completely before cutting and serving.

Other Goodness You Need to Know!

Brötchen (Hard Rolls)

2½ to 3 cups all-purpose flour
1 package active dry yeast
1 tsp. sugar
1 tsp. salt
1 tsp. oil
1 cup lukewarm water
1 egg white

- Pour 2½ cups flour in a large bowl and form a well in the middle.
- In the well, mix the yeast, sugar, and 2 tbsp. of the lukewarm water. Sprinkle a little flour over the mixture.
- Cover bowl and let the mixture rise in a warm place for 15 minutes.
- Add the remaining water and oil and knead the yeast mixture and flour together until smooth. Add remaining ½ cup of flour if needed.

- Cover the bowl and let dough rise at a warm place for about 1 hour until it doubles in size.
- Punch down and divide the dough in 12 parts.
- Shape into 12 rolls and place them 3 inches apart on a parchment lined cookie sheet.
- Cover and let rise until rolls for about 30 minutes until the rolls are doubled in size.
- Preheat oven to 450° F.
- Beat egg white with 1 tsp. water and brush on rolls.
- Bake for 15 to 20 minutes until golden brown.
- The rolls should have a crispy outside and a chewy inside.

Roggenbrot (Rye Bread)

2 packages active dry yeast
½ cup lukewarm water
1½ cups lukewarm milk
2 tbsp. sugar
1 tsp. salt
½ cup molasses
2 tbsp. butter
3¼ cups rye flour, unsifted
2½cups bread flour, unsifted

- Dissolve yeast in water.
- In a large bowl, mix milk, sugar, and salt.
- Use a mixer to beat in molasses, yeast mixture, and 1 cup of rye flour.
- With a wooden spoon, mix in the remaining rye flour.
- Stir in bread flour until dough is stiff enough to knead by hand.
- Knead for 5 to 10 minutes adding bread flour as needed until the dough does not stick to hands.
- Cover dough and let rise in a warm place for 1½ hour.
- Punch down and divide to form 2 loaves.

- Let the loaves rise on a greased baking sheet for 1½ hour.
- Preheat oven to 375° F.
- Brush loaves with cold water and bake for 35 minutes.
- Remove bread from oven and knock on the bottom of the loaf. If it sounds hollow, the bread is perfectly done. If not, the bread might need 5 more minutes of baking.

Kartoffelknödel (Potato Dumplings)

7 baking medium baking potatoes
¼ cup all-purpose flour
2 eggs
1 tsp. salt
¼ tsp. ground nutmeg
2 tbsp. butter
3 slices bread, cut into cubes

- Cook potatoes in water until tender.
- Cover and refrigerate for 24 hours.
- Peel cooked potatoes and mash thoroughly.
- Combine potatoes, flour, eggs, salt, and nutmeg to form a firm paste.
- If mixture is too wet, add flour as needed.
- Melt butter in a skillet, add bread cubes, and fry until golden brown.
- Split potato dough into 10 parts and form into dumplings. Place a few bread cubes in the center of each dumpling.
- The outside of each dumpling should be smooth and solid.
- Bring a large pot of water with 2 tbsp. of salt to boil.
- Add dumplings, one at a time, and simmer uncovered for 15 minutes.
- Dumplings are done when they float to the on top.

- Remove dumplings with a slotted spoon and drain well.
- Dumplings taste best with a gravy dish.

Semmelknödel (Bread Dumplings)

10 hard rolls
1 - 2 cups warm milk
½ cup bacon diced
1 tbsp. butter, softened
1 small onion, diced
1 tbsp. parsley flakes
3 eggs
½ tsp. salt
¼ tsp. pepper

- Cube hard rolls and place in a large bowl. Set aside overnight to dry.
- Soak bread in warm milk. Bread should be moist but not soggy.
- Fry onions and bacon in butter until onions are tender.
- Add bacon-onion mixture, parsley flakes, eggs, salt, and pepper to the bread and stir until well combined.
- Bring a large pot of water with 2 tbsp. of salt to a boil.
- Add dumplings, one at a time, and simmer uncovered for 20 minutes.
- Dumplings are done when they float to the on top.
- Remove dumplings with a slotted spoon and drain well.

Kartoffelpfannkuchen (Potato Pancakes)

We usually serve these with applesauce as a side dish with soups.

2 lb. Potatoes, peeled
1 cup all-purpose flour
2 tsp. salt
3 eggs
Vegetable oil for frying

- Grate potatoes by hand in a large bowl.
- Add flour, salt, and eggs and mix well.
- Heat oil in a large skillet until hot.
- About ½ inch of oil should cover the bottom of the skillet.
- Drop about ¼ cup of potato batter per pancake into skillet and fry until golden brown on both sides.
- Drain on a paper towel.
- Continue until all potato batter is used.

Griessklösschen (Farina Dumplings)

1 egg, beaten
1 tbsp. butter, softened
Pinch of salt
¼ cup Cream of Wheat of Farina
Chicken broth

- Mix egg, butter, salt, and farina well.
- Refrigerate at least 2 hours.
- Bring a medium pot of chicken broth to a boil.
- Make miniature dumplings the size of a teaspoon.
- Drop dumplings gently into the boiling broth.
- Simmer for 5 minutes.
- Serve in the broth or in any other soup.

Rotkraut (Red Cabbage)

1 medium head red cabbage, finely chopped
2 granny smith apples, chopped
1 small onion, chopped
4 whole cloves
3 tbsp. vinegar
2 tbsp. sugar
2 tbsp. oil
2 tbsp. all-purpose flour
Water

- Combine cabbage, apples, onions, cloves, vinegar, sugar, and oil in a large pot.
- Add enough water to cover the bottom of the pot.
- Bring to a boil and simmer for about 20 minutes until tender.
- Dust with flour and stir well.
- Taste and to determine if more sugar is needed.
- Serve with dumplings or potatoes and meat dishes.

Rezeptverzeichnis 1 (German Recipe Index)

Kartoffelpfannkuchen (Potato Pancakes) 98
Kartoffelsalat 1 (Potato Salad 1) 50
Kartoffelsalat 2 (Potato Salad 2) 51
Kässesuppe (Cheese Soup) 27
Kokos Makronen (Coconut Macaroons) 43
Königsberger Klopse (Königsberger meatballs) 65
Königssuppe (Kings Soup) 15
Kräuterlamm (Herbed Lamb) 16
Krautrouladen (cabbage rolls) 22
Krautsuppe (Cabbage Soup) 58
Kreppel 9
Kroketten (Potato Tots) 17
Leberklösschen (Liver Dumplings) 66
Linsensuppe mit Frankfurter
(Lentil Soup with Frankfurter) 59
Maibowle (May Punch) 19
Mandelflammeri (Almond Pudding) 77
Marmorkuchen (Marble Cake) 88
Martinsgans mit Apfelfüllung
(Goose with Apple Stuffing) 31
Marzipan 37
Mehlsuppe (Flour Soup) 60
Nudelsalat (Noodle Salad) 51
Ochsenschwanzsuppe (Oxtail Soup) 47
Ofen Nudelsuppe (Oven Noodle Soup) 60
Pilze in Sahnesosse (Mushrooms in Cream Sauce) 67
Rehschmortopf (Venison Casserole) 67
Rindergulasch (Beef goulash) 68
Rindfleischrouladen (Beef rolls) 71
Rindfleischsalat (Beef Salad) 54
Rippenspeer (Pork ribs) 69
Roastbraten mit Pilzfüllung
(Roast with Mushroom Stuffing) 70
Roggenbrot (Rye Bread) 95
Rote Grütze (Red Grits) 24
Rotkraut (Red Cabbage) 99
Rustikale Birnentarte mit Spätem Riesling
(Rustic Pear Tart with Late Harvest Riesling) 28

Sauerbraten (Sour Roast) 72
Sauerkrautsalat 55
Schneeflocken (Snowflakes) 44
Schnitzel (Veal Cutlet) 75
Schokoladencreme (Chocolate Cream) 78
Schusterpfanne (Shoemaker pot) 73
Schwarzwälder Kirschtorte (Black Forest Torte) 89
Schweinefilet (Pork Tenderloins) 74
Semmelauflauf (Almond Soufflés) 78
Semmelknödel (Bread Dumplings) 97
Sieben Kräuter Suppe (Seven Herb Soup) 11
Silvester Bowle (New Year's Eve Punch) 48
Streuselkuchen (Crumb Cake) 91
Strohsuppe (Straw Soup) 61
Unser Familien Salat (Our Family Salad) 52
Vanillecreme (Vanilla Cream) 79
Vanillekipferl (Vanilla Crescent) 43
Viel Glück Plätzchen (Good Luck Cookies) 49
Weihnachtssterne (Christmas Stars) 45
Weincreme (Wine Cream) 80
Weinerntesuppe (Vintage Soup) 61
Weintraubentorte (Grape Torte) 92
Wurstsalat (Meat Salad) 52
Zigeunerschnitzel (Gypsy Veal Cutlet) 76
Zimtsterne (Cinnamon Stars) 42
Zitronenkuchen (Lemon Cake) 93
Zwetschgenknödel (Plum Dumplings) 80

40228836R00059

Made in the USA
San Bernardino, CA
15 October 2016